CGP

11+ English Comprehension

For **GL** Assessment

When it comes to 11+ preparation, nothing beats practice — and this CGP book is full of the best English Comprehension practice you'll find, all for ages 10-11.

It starts with questions that focus on one topic at a time, so children can get to grips with the crucial Comprehension skills for GL 11+ English. Once they're confident, there's a selection of mixed-topic Assessment Tests to help them get used to the style of the real 11+ papers.

We've also included fully explained answers at the back of the book. Everything you need!

Unlock your Online Edition

Just scan the QR code below or go to **cgpbooks.co.uk/extras** and enter this code!

3826 9601 8854 9382

Online Edition

By the way, this code only works for one person. If somebody else has used this book before you, they might have already claimed the code.

Practice Book – Ages 10-11
with Assessment Tests

How to use this Practice Book

This book is divided into two parts — themed question practice and assessment tests.
There are answers and detailed explanations at the back of the book.

Themed question practice

- Each page contains practice questions divided by topic. Use these pages to work out your child's strengths and the areas they find tricky. The questions get harder down each page.

- Your child can use the smiley face tick boxes to evaluate how confident they feel with each topic.

Assessment tests

- The second half of the book contains seven assessment tests, each with two comprehension texts and a matching set of questions. They take a similar form to the real test.

- You can print multiple-choice answer sheets so your child can practise the tests as if they're sitting the real thing — visit cgpbooks.co.uk/11plus/answer-sheets or scan the QR code. → **Answer Sheets**

- Use the printable answer sheets if you want your child to do each test more than once.

- If you want to give your child timed practice, give them a time limit of 28 minutes for each test, and ask them to work as quickly and carefully as they can.

- The tests get harder from 1-7, so don't be surprised if your child finds the later ones more tricky.

- Your child should aim for a mark of around 85% (24 questions correct) in each test. If they score less than this, use their results to work out the areas they need more practice on.

- If they haven't managed to finish the test in time, they need to work on increasing their speed, whereas if they have made a lot of mistakes, they need to work more carefully.

- Keep track of your child's scores using the progress chart at the back of the book.

Published by CGP

Editors:

Claire Boulter, Tom Carney, Josie Gilbert, Georgina Paxman and Kirsty Sweetman

With thanks to Catherine Heygate for the proofreading.
With thanks to Hannah Wilkie and Beth Linnane for the copyright research.

For copyright reasons, this book is not for sale in the USA, Canada or the Philippines.

Please note that CGP is not associated with GL Assessment in any way.
This book does not include any official questions and is not endorsed by GL Assessment.

A note for teachers, parents and caregivers
Just something to bear in mind if you're choosing further reading for 10-11 year olds — all the extracts in this book are suitable for children of this age, but we can't vouch for the full texts they're taken from, or other works by the same authors.

Extract on page 32: 'Savi and the Memory Keeper' by Bijal Vachharajani.
Reproduced with permission from Hachette India Book Publishing
Extract on page 47: 'A Master of Djinn' by P. Djèlí Clark.
© Reproduced with the permission of Little Brown Book Group through PLSclear

ISBN: 978 1 83774 163 2
Printed by Elanders Ltd, Newcastle upon Tyne
Clipart from Corel®

Based on the classic CGP style created by Richard Parsons.

Contents

Tick off the check box for each topic as you go along.

Finding Facts

Read the passage below, then answer the questions that follow.

Although they are widespread throughout the UK, kingfishers are notoriously shy birds. Despite their brightly coloured orange and blue feathers, their timidity and modest size make them easy to miss — at just 16 cm in length, they are only marginally bigger than a robin. However, if you're lucky you might occasionally glimpse one
5   perching on a low-hanging branch alongside a river, waiting patiently for its prey.

As their name suggests, kingfishers predominantly feed on small fish, which they catch by diving into slow-moving water at an impressive speed of up to 40 km per hour. Their long, narrow beaks pierce the water's surface without a splash, meaning their prey are not alerted to their presence until it is too late.

10   During harsh winters, freshwater freezes and kingfishers struggle to find food. When the availability of aquatic food sources is limited, they may resort to feeding on beetles and other insects. Alternatively, some kingfishers survive by migrating to estuaries or coastal areas, where water is less likely to freeze.

For each statement below, write down whether it is true or false.

1.   Kingfishers are the same size as robins.   _____

2.   Kingfishers can be seen near waterways.   _____

3.   Kingfishers only eat fish.   _____

4.   All kingfishers relocate in winter.   _____

Write down one piece of evidence from the text to support each of the following statements.

5.   It is quite rare to see a kingfisher.

_____

6.   Kingfishers move very quickly.

_____

7.   There is often less food available for kingfishers in winter.

/ 7

_____

Finding Facts

Read the passage below, then answer the questions that follow.
Underline the correct option for each question.

Born in New York in 1901, Adelaide Hall was a popular singer and entertainer. She is widely recognised as an early pioneer of 'scat singing' — an improvised style of jazz singing where the voice mimics an instrument. As the daughter of a music teacher, Hall's interest in music was fostered from an early age, and throughout her youth she performed at local

5 events alongside her sister. Hall's first Broadway performance was in the African-American musical 'Shuffle Along' in 1921.

Following success on both sides of the Atlantic, Hall finally settled in London with her husband in 1938. Together, they opened a nightclub in London's Mayfair, and Hall also landed a starring role in a West End musical. During the Second World War, Hall hosted

10 her own radio show and even performed in underground shelters to help boost Londoners' morale.

In the years after the war, Hall's popularity fluctuated but never entirely died out. Over the remainder of her career, she recorded the soundtrack to a number of films and appeared on several TV shows, becoming one of the most highly paid entertainers of her time.

1. Hall was born in the:

    A 18th century.   B 19th century.   C 20th century.   D 21st century.

2. Which of the following facts about scat singing is not mentioned in the text?

    A What it sounds like   B What genre of music it is   C When it was first introduced

3. Which of the following statements is true?

    A Hall was the only scat singer during her lifetime.
    B Hall had a career in the USA and the UK.
    C Hall performed solo at small events as a child.

Hint: Read all of the answer options before deciding which one to underline.

4. During the Second World War, Hall:

    A built shelters.   B moved to London.   C lifted spirits.   D threw parties.

5. After the Second World War, Hall:

    A continued to be successful in her career.
    B became steadily less popular over time.
    C became the highest paid performer of all time.

/ 5

Section One — Information and Ideas

Finding Facts

Read the passage below, then answer the questions that follow.

After ten strained minutes, Tia and Iris eventually saw eye to eye on where to pitch their shabby tent. Tia had initially proposed this trip several months ago, after stumbling across the tent in her cluttered garage while trying to unearth her prized telescope. What she had failed to reveal at the time was that she had never been camping before. Now

5 though, as she grappled clumsily with a tent pole, that lack of experience was all too clear.

Iris sulked as she watched Tia unfurl their moth-eaten home for the weekend, then stomped off to collect firewood. Trying not to let Iris's lack of enthusiasm faze her, Tia busied herself decoding the tattered instructions that were just about legible in the fading light. After what felt like an eternity, but in reality was only half an hour, she had erected their temporary abode.

10 A colossal yawn escaped from Tia's mouth, and she crawled into the tent. As she unrolled her sleeping bag, she was startled by a cry from outside. She scrambled out to see Iris peering upwards, her arms full of sticks and her face a mask of wonder. Tia followed her gaze: overhead, countless streaks of light illuminated the pitch-black sky.

Tia smothered a grin. Perhaps seeing a meteor shower would convince Iris that camping

15 wasn't such an appalling idea after all.

Write down the answer to each question below.

1. Whose idea was it to go camping? _____

2. What was Tia looking for in the garage? _____

3. How long are Tia and Iris planning to camp for? _____

4. How many minutes does it take Tia to pitch the tent? _____

Write down one piece of evidence from the text to support each of the following statements.

5. Their tent isn't in very good condition.

_____

6. The tent instructions are difficult to read.

_____

7. There are lots of meteors in the sky.

/ 7

_____

Finding Facts

Read the poem below, then answer the questions that follow.
Underline the correct option for each question.

Our journey dawns as the sun descends,
Bright scarlet hues such bewitching jewels.

The train thunders through emerald meadows,
Holding us captive while Nature — she glows.

5 Starlings swoop, twisting and whirling,
A shifting cloud of pearl-like flecks.

A dozen skittish deer frolic to our right,
Far too swift they escape from our sight.

Snow-capped mountains slide out of view,
10 Milk-white pyramids framing the horizon.

Glistening softly in the dying light,
A majestic landscape shining so bright.

Forlorn to know that this journey will cease,
And bring to an end our treasured peace.

15 For Nature has shown us precious delights,
But we must go back to dull city sights.

1. What time of day is it when the train journey begins?

   A Morning   **B** Afternoon   **C** Evening   **D** Night

2. Which colour is not mentioned in the poem?

   A Blue   **B** Red   **C** White   **D** Green

3. Why doesn't the narrator see the deer for very long?

   A The narrator is distracted by the mountains.
   B The deer are shy and try to hide.
   C The deer move quickly out of sight.

4. What does line 9 reveal about the mountains?

   A They are completely covered in snow.
   B Only the summits are covered in snow.
   C The summits used to be covered in snow.

5. Which of the following does the narrator not mention?

   A How they feel about the journey ending.
   B Where their journey ends.
   C Where in the train they are sitting.
   D What types of landscape they pass through.

/ 5

Section One — Information and Ideas

Finding Hidden Facts

Read the passage below, then answer the questions that follow.

Mia settled back on the sofa, wrapped her blanket tightly around herself and basked in the thin rays of sunlight just starting to filter through the broken blinds. A whole day to herself! She couldn't remember when she'd last spent time downstairs without her housemate, Reece, complaining at her — he seemed to find a new thing to grumble about
5 every day. Luckily, he was away this weekend visiting his parents, and Mia planned to take full advantage of the short respite.

Just as she was about to turn the TV on, there was a loud knock at the front door. Mia gave a deep sigh and reluctantly untangled herself from the blanket. She padded down the hallway, instinctively avoiding the creaky floorboard. Absentmindedly, she performed the ritual
10 necessary to open the warped door — push with a shoulder, twist the latch, gentle kick to the base — and it sprang open. In front of her was the largest bouquet of flowers she'd ever seen.

It had been carefully placed on the doorstep, but there was nobody around. Frowning, Mia looked up and down the road. The usual steady stream of traffic rumbled past, and in the distance she could hear the cries of market vendors and the shouts of children arriving at
15 school — but the mysterious delivery person had vanished into thin air.

Draw lines to connect each detail from the text to how it makes Mia feel.

1. She is alone for the day.

2. Her house is run down.

3. There is a knock at her door.

4. Flowers are delivered to her house.

Irritated

Happy

Bored

Confused

Unconcerned

You will have one answer option left over.

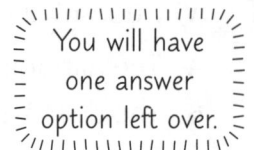

Underline the word from the brackets that best completes the sentences below. Give one reason why you chose each of your answers.

5. Mia's housemate makes her feel _____. (**forgetful   annoyed   lonely**)

Reason: _____

6. Mia lives in _____. (**the countryside   a town   a bungalow**)

Reason: _____

/ 6

Finding Hidden Facts

Read the passage below, then answer the questions that follow.
Underline the correct option for each question.

During the third hour of the marathon, Jamal began to wonder if he would ever actually reach the finish line. The heavy rhythm of his feet on the ground was starting to falter, and every part of his body was screaming at him. He glimpsed the flags of a water station up ahead, nearly blending in with the clear summer sky, and navigated his way through the rest of
5 the unfortunate souls who'd signed up for this ordeal. A smiling woman at the counter handed him a bottle.

"You've got this! Just keep going!" Jamal barely heard the words as he opened the bottle and emptied it over his head. Something in her expression, however, made him think about his mum. She was the one who'd encouraged him to take part in this, and who had been endlessly
10 supportive throughout his training. Jamal knew she'd be waiting for him at the end, probably with a homemade banner and a bag full of snacks. The thought of getting to celebrate with her filled Jamal with a new rush of energy. He smiled back at the woman.

"Thanks — I'll see you on the other side!" He turned away, ignoring the burning in his legs and lungs, and rejoined the crowd of people all steadily working towards a common goal.

1. What colour are the flags signalling the water station?
   A White   B Orange   C Blue   D Grey

2. Why does Jamal call the other runners "unfortunate souls" (line 5)?
   A Because they don't have anyone waiting for them at the finish line.
   B Because he has overtaken them and will get to collect his bottle of water first.
   C Because he is struggling with the marathon and assumes other runners must feel the same.

3. Jamal "barely heard" (line 7) the woman at the water station because he was:
   A daydreaming.   B overheating.   C thirsty.   D impolite.

4. How do you think the woman at the water station looks at Jamal?
   A Reassuringly   B Insightfully   C Pityingly   D Timidly

5. At the end of the extract, how do you think Jamal is feeling about the marathon?
   A Pessimistic because he's still tired.
   B Confident because he thinks he'll finish.
   C Dismissive because he thinks it'll be easy.

/ 5

Section One — Information and Ideas

Finding Hidden Facts

The Angel of the North is an icon of the British skyline — an imposing statue designed by sculptor Antony Gormley and constructed between 1994 and 1998. Standing as a silent guardian over the town of Gateshead, the Angel is modelled on Gormley himself and was commissioned to act as a landmark for those entering the area by car or train. Its wings are
5 tilted forwards at a 3.5 degree angle, intended to create the impression of an embrace.

The Angel stands 20 metres tall, with another 20 metres of support underground. It is made from a special type of steel — this steel weathers over time, producing a rusty hue. A team of engineers worked on the details of the structure to ensure that it would be stable, and the final construction can withstand winds of over 100 miles per hour.

10 Multiple organisations, including local, national and international groups, helped to fund the project. Initially, there were some doubts over its installation, as people were concerned about how it would look and the impact it could have on traffic or radio signals. However, it has since become a part of the North East's identity and one of the most recognisable sculptures in the country. Residents have adopted the statue as a symbol of hope and
15 optimism, while for the millions of people who pass it each year, it is a spectacular sight.

Write down one phrase from the text to support each of the following inferences.

1. The Angel is visible from nearby roads.

   _____

2. The Angel was designed to change colour as it aged.

   _____

Underline the word from the brackets that best completes the sentences below. Give one reason why you chose each of your answers.

3. The Angel has a _____ appearance. **(distinctive   childlike   disruptive)**

   Reason: _____

4. The writer has a _____ opinion of the Angel. **(neutral   critical   positive)**

   Reason: _____

/ 4

Finding Hidden Facts

Read the poem below, then answer the questions that follow.
Underline the correct option for each question.

It glided in above the waves,
Untethered from the rise and fall.
The ship that took them to their graves
Is now returned and standing tall.

5   The age-old legend clearly said
Not one of us should make a sound
And voice our sorrow and our dread,
Or we too would run aground.

The ship gave off a ghostly glow,
10   Our faces lit a shade of green.
The grief inside began to grow
As we beheld the eerie scene.

The captain then emerged on deck
And turned her face towards the land
15   Where her ship was doomed to wreck
And wash up in pieces on the sand.

Countless figures gathered round her
Gripping hands as the sea surged high
Bravely faced their fate, did not stir
20   As the waves reached for the sky.

Our eyes stung with unshed tears
As the ship disappeared from sight
The sea around turned calm and clear
And we sailed on through the night.

1. Which of these statements about the ghost ship is true?
    A It moves with the waves in the sea.
    B It ran aground on a calm day.
    C It was wrecked many years ago.

2. Why don't the sailors make any noise when they see the ghost ship?
    A They believe there is a curse on the ship.
    B They do not want to wake the captain up.
    C They are trying to avoid hitting the ship.

3. Which of the following statements is false?
    A The ghost ship has a large crew.
    B The ghost ship sinks within sight of the shore.
    C The crew try to steer the ghost ship out to sea.

4. Which of the following best describes how the sailors feel about seeing the ghost ship?
    A Full of pity for the crew of the ship.
    B Full of wonder at what they have seen.
    C Full of fear that the ghosts might follow them.

/ 4

Interpreting Quotes

Read the passage below, then answer the questions that follow.

Elias tore along the endless, winding corridors, sweat surging off his brow.

"Not today," he gasped. "Not again."

Rounding a tight bend, he pirouetted between huddles of pupils, shimmied through gaps a half-starved rat would think ambitious, and vaulted over a toppled locker like it wasn't there.

5 The slap of straining soles on worn tiles split the air at regular, frantic intervals, piercing the incessant murmuring that filled the halls. Driven by desperation, Elias ran on.

As his destination loomed into view, a flicker of hope danced in Elias's heart before being abruptly snuffed out. He skidded to a halt. The door was closed. The lights were off. He was too late. The crushing weight of despair buckled his knees as a sob rose in his now-hoarse

10 throat. *I'm finished,* he thought to himself as he struggled to stay standing. *I'm too late.*

The door gave an asthmatic wheeze as it opened.

"Ah, Mr Idi — are you here to hand in your homework? You're in luck: I was just leaving."

Write down one quote from the text to support each of the following statements.

1. Elias is running as fast as he can.

_____

2. Elias moves nimbly.

_____

3. Elias feels optimistic about arriving in time.

_____

Write down what you think each quote below means.

4. "gaps a half-starved rat would think ambitious" (lines 3-4)

_____

5. "despair buckled his knees" (line 9)

_____

6. "The door gave an asthmatic wheeze" (line 11)

/ 6

_____

Interpreting Quotes

> Read the passage below, then answer the questions that follow.
> Underline the correct option for each question.

Carbonara. An iconic Italian dish, adored by millions all around the world. But just how Italian is it? And is it as much of an 'old classic' as people think?

While it might seem like this creamy and comforting meal has been around forever, some believe that it only sprang into existence during World War II. Supporters of this theory say
5   that American soldiers offered their rations of bacon and eggs to Italian chefs in return for a "spaghetti breakfast", and carbonara was the fortuitous result.

Others suspect that the dish has its origins firmly in Italian hands, with the meal originally being prepared outside over open fires by men who produced charcoal. Devotees of this origin story are inclined to stress the similarity between the Italian word for charcoal workers
10 ('carbonari') and the name of the dish.

Others argue that the charcoal industry played no role in the development of carbonara. Instead, they contend that the name is a nod to the abundance of black pepper in the recipe, because the black specks resemble coal dust.

Whichever theory you believe, one thing is generally agreed upon by all — for a dish with
15 only a handful of key ingredients, the whole is greater than the sum of its parts.

1. What does the phrase "adored by millions" (line 1) mean?

   A well-known   **B** well-liked   **C** well-made   **D** well-founded

2. "carbonara was the fortuitous result" (line 6). This suggests that the creation of carbonara:

   A should be credited to the skill of the Italian chefs.
   B may never be traced back to any single person.
   C resulted from a lucky combination of circumstances.

3. What does "inclined to stress" (line 9) suggest about supporters of this theory?

   A They tend to worry.   **B** They emphasise a point.   **C** They stretch the truth.

4. The phrase "the abundance of black pepper" (line 12) refers to what quality of the pepper?

   A the amount   **B** the size   **C** the smell   **D** the cost

5. "the whole is greater than the sum of its parts" (line 15) suggests that carbonara:

   A is tastier than its individual ingredients.
   B is so simple that anyone can make it.
   C is surprisingly rich and heavy.

/ 5

Section One — Information and Ideas

Word Meanings

Read the poem below, then answer the questions that follow.

The Earth was formed of rocks and dust
Irresistible attraction, swirling chance
They came together to build a home
And the stars watched.

5   The spark of life took root on Earth
Primitive plants, clumsy creatures
Building on what came before
And the stars watched.

Conflict followed in mankind's wake
10 Clashing views, futile feuds
From swords and spears to lethal words
And the stars watched.

But magic was created, too
Inspiring science, exquisite art
15 A melody that all could sing
And the stars watched.

We'll take our leave — someday, somehow
Something new, an unknown fate
The Earth uninhabited; silent, still
20 And the stars will watch.

Draw lines to connect each word from the text with the word that has the closest meaning.

1. Irresistible (line 2)

2. Primitive (line 6)

3. Futile (line 10)

4. Inspiring (line 14)

5. Exquisite (line 14)

Pointless

Beautiful

Stimulating

Basic

Refreshing

Overpowering

You will have one answer option left over.

Write down one word from the text that means the same as each of the following words.

6. Ungainly _____

7. Deadly _____

8. Billowing _____

9. Deserted _____

10. Destiny _____

/ 10

Word Meanings

> Read the passage below, then answer the questions that follow.
> Underline the correct option for each question.

"The cameras have been deactivated — now's the time!" came Oscar's voice through the earpiece, full of exhilaration. Tasha nodded sharply to her two companions, all of them clad in black, and motioned for them to move into the corridor. Keeping close to the wall, the three figures hurried stealthily to the next turn. Tasha stole a quick glance around the

5 corner and let out a sigh of relief.

The pair of guards outside the vault's door were slumped on the floor in a stupor, just as Oscar had promised they would be. Tasha stepped up to the tarnished control panel on the door, causing one of the guards to stir slightly as she brushed past him.

"Don't worry," she said sympathetically. "We'll be gone soon."

10 The door required an eight-digit number, but Tasha knew exactly what it would be. She warily typed out the date that her money was stolen from her, relishing the moment. Today, justice would be served.

1. Which of these words is closest in meaning to "exhilaration" (line 2)?

   A Exhaustion   **B** Anxiety   **C** Excitement   **D** Urgency

2. What is meant by the word "clad" (line 3)?

   A Stylish   **B** Dressed   **C** Disguised   **D** Camouflaged

3. Which of these words is closest in meaning to "stealthily" (line 4)?

   A Quickly   **B** Calmly   **C** Deliberately   **D** Secretively

4. What is meant by the word "tarnished" (line 7)?

   A Metal   **B** Discoloured   **C** Polished   **D** Ancient

5. The word "warily" (line 11) could be most accurately replaced by:

   A casually.   **B** forcefully.   **C** slowly.   **D** cautiously.

6. Which of these words could most accurately replace "relishing" (line 11)?

   A enjoying   **B** regretting   **C** prolonging   **D** remembering

/ 6

Word Types

> Read the passage below, then answer the questions that follow.

Although a number of animals can glide, bats are the only mammal that can achieve true flight. In fact, some species of bat can reach speeds of nearly 100 miles per hour. When flying at such astonishing speeds, a bat's heart can beat 1000 times per minute.

5   The majority of bat species use echoes in order to navigate their environment. Sound waves issued from their nose or mouth bounce off objects around them, providing them with an accurate picture of their surroundings. This clever technique, called 'echolocation', allows bats to successfully detect the insects they feed on, even in complete darkness.

Like bees and butterflies, some species of bats are also pollinators. This means that these bats play a key role in the reproduction of plants, which is vital for sustaining life on Earth.

10   Unfortunately, bats face a number of threats to their existence, including habitat loss, which has caused their numbers to fall. Since they generally have just one baby each year, bat numbers can take a long time to recover once the population has declined.

Hint: If you're not too sure on your technical terms, turn to p.65 to have a look at the glossary.

> Write down whether the word in bold is a verb, an adjective, a noun or an adverb.

1.   "the only mammal that can **achieve** true flight" (lines 1-2)   _____

2.   "even in complete **darkness**" (line 7)   _____

3.   "they **generally** have just one baby each year" (line 11)   _____

4.   "bat numbers can take a **long** time to recover" (line 12)   _____

> Underline the word in each phrase that matches the word type in brackets.

5.   "allows bats to successfully detect the insects they feed on" (line 7)   **(adverb)**

6.   "bounce off objects around them" (line 5)   **(concrete noun)**

7.   "vital for sustaining life on Earth" (line 9)   **(proper noun)**

8.   "which has caused their numbers to fall" (line 11)   **(preposition)**

/ 8

Word Types

> Read the passage below, then answer the questions that follow.
> Underline the correct option for each question.

While frantically whisking a bowl of chocolate buttercream, I heard a sob. Glancing over my shoulder, I saw Lyn failing to stifle tears as she peered into the oven in disbelief.

"What's wrong?" I enquired, with a degree of apprehension.

"It's the pastry," Lyn cried out in an exasperated tone. "It isn't rising!"

5   I was aware that our decision to make pastry swans for Mum's birthday was an ambitious one. However, I thought that our deep-rooted love of baking would triumph over all.

For as long as I can remember, I've relished a cosy Sunday afternoon spent whipping up fairy cakes or a delectable batch of chocolate brownies, with the radio murmuring quietly in the background. Making pastry swans,
10 unsurprisingly, was proving a far cry from following those simple recipes.

After a few seconds of confusion, I noticed the oven temperature dial...

"The oven is only set to 50 °C," I said evenly, hiding my frustration to spare Lyn's feelings.

"Oh no!" Lyn replied despairingly. "I guess the swans will be ugly ducklings instead..."

1.   "Glancing over my shoulder" (lines 1-2). Which of these words is a preposition?
   A Glancing   **B** over   **C** my   **D** shoulder

2.   What type of word is "stifle" (line 2)?
   A Adjective   **B** Verb   **C** Adverb   **D** Abstract noun

3.   What type of words are these?
   birthday   **love**   **confusion**
   A Collective nouns   **B** Concrete nouns   **C** Proper nouns   **D** Abstract nouns

4.   What type of word is "aware" (line 5)?
   A Proper noun   **B** Adverb   **C** Adjective   **D** Verb

5.   What type of word is "only" (line 12)?
   A Adjective   **B** Preposition   **C** Pronoun   **D** Adverb

/ 5

Abbreviations

Read the passage below, then answer the questions that follow.

Dear Diary,

Today, I learnt all about Antarctica. I've summed up all my favourite facts below:

- Antarctica contains approx 70% of the world's fresh water.

- It is the driest, coldest, windiest, highest and iciest continent on Earth.

5   - The vast majority of Antarctica is covered by ice — it's over 4.5 km deep in places.

- Mt Vinson, with a summit 4892 m above sea level, is the continent's tallest peak.

- Antarctica experienced the coldest temp ever recorded in July 1983.
  (Thermostats plunged to –89 °C at Vostok Research Stn.)

- The first person to step foot on Antarctica was John Davis, a US-born explorer, in 1821.

10   - In the late 18th century, Capt James Cook spent three years searching for Antarctica.
  (Cook came within 80 mi of the Antarctic coastline but failed to find it.)

- Antarctica has no permanent residents, but there are several research facilities (some of
  which are funded by the UK govt) that host scientists from around the world.

- Antarctica is becoming a popular tourist destination, with around 100 000 visitors per yr.

15   - There may be up to half a million penguins living on the Antarctic continent.

Write out the full word for each abbreviation listed below.

1.   approx (line 3)　　_____

2.   km (line 5)　　_____

3.   Mt (line 6)　　_____

4.   temp (line 7)　　_____

5.   Capt (line 10)　　_____

6.   mi (line 11)　　_____

7.   govt (line 13)　　_____

8.   yr (line 14)　　_____

/ 8

Alliteration and Onomatopoeia

Read the poem below, then answer the questions that follow.
Underline the correct option for each question.

Cactus: champion of contradictions.
You are life in the death of the dusty desert,
You hoard your cherished sap inside stout,
Springy arms, outstretched for endless hours.
5 Decades of dozing dullness. Watching, waiting
For the historic moment to arrive.
It's here.
Roiling, rumbling, constantly stirring
Clouds darken the dunes; thunder cracks the sky.
10 A whisper of water, a roar, then a
Downpour — dry earth gulping, jewelled drops
Glistening as shallow roots unfold.

Liquid lifeblood flows, oozes in veins
That rouse from slumber, sputter awake
15 and recall their purpose. Now nourished,
A radiant rose bursts into bloom:
The gentle joy of blushing blossom
Nestled amongst sharp, spiked sentries.

1. Which of the following phrases is an example of alliteration?

   A hoard your   **B** whisper of water   **C** It's here   **D** gulping, jewelled

2. Which of the following words is an example of onomatopoeia?

   A rumbling   **B** Downpour   **C** flows   **D** Nestled

3. Which of the following phrases is an example of alliteration?

   A Cactus: champion   **B** cherished sap   **C** endless hours   **D** radiant rose

4. Which of the following words is an example of onomatopoeia?

   A Springy   **B** sputter   **C** bloom   **D** spiked

5. Which of the following phrases is an example of alliteration?

   A jewelled drops   **B** constantly stirring   **C** dry earth   **D** gentle joy

6. Which of the following words is an example of Onomatopoeia?

   A stout   **B** gulping   **C** Glistening   **D** slumber

/ 6

Section Two — Writers' Techniques

Imagery

This is a retelling of a story from Chinese folklore.

Many moons ago, it is believed that the Jade Emperor, Lord of Heaven, descended to Earth in disguise to seek out an animal companion. He considered humans far too fickle and untrustworthy, changing like the wind whenever it suited them.

Three animals presented themselves to the masked Emperor: a monkey, a fox and a
5 rabbit. Falling to his knees, the Emperor imitated a starving beggar.

"Please help me, for the earthquake in my stomach is too much to bear!" he cried.

Fast as arrows, the trio of animals shot off to gather provisions. The monkey harvested fruits and nuts from the generous forest canopy; the fox plucked plump fish from the stream; but the rabbit only managed a small, rather glum pile of grass.

10 As realisation dawned like the sun on the rabbit — *humans can't sustain themselves with grass* — it sprang into action. With nerves of steel and a heart of gold, it leapt over the startled animals and the masked Emperor, towards a fire that licked hungrily at the air.

"Eat me, so you can survive!" it declared, running as fast as it could.

Realising that the rabbit's spirit was as pure as heaven itself, the Emperor scooped up the
15 noble creature before it could reach the fire. He carried his new companion up to the moon, where he gave it a great responsibility: crafting potions of immortality.

To this day, some say that you can see the honourable rabbit outlined on the full moon.

Write down whether each phrase below contains a simile, a metaphor or personification.

1. "changing like the wind whenever it suited them" (line 3) _____

2. "the earthquake in my stomach" (line 6) _____

3. "Fast as arrows, the trio of animals shot off" (line 7) _____

4. "fruits and nuts from the generous forest canopy" (line 8) _____

5. "realisation dawned like the sun on the rabbit" (line 10) _____

6. "nerves of steel and a heart of gold" (line 11) _____

7. "a fire that licked hungrily at the air" (line 12) _____

8. "the rabbit's spirit was as pure as heaven itself" (line 14) _____

/ 8

Imagery

Read the poem below, then answer the questions that follow.
Underline the correct option for each question.

We walk straight into its jaws,
As the queue snakes slowly on.
Push out of mind the fear that gnaws,
For we've missed our chance to run.

5   Clamber in and settle down,
Steel arms give a chill embrace.
Resist the fresh new urge to frown,
Like runners in a one-horse race.

We're off — slowly rolling, coasting,
10 Carted along the monstrous spine.
Tipped back, angled up and blinking,
Climbing high to heavens divine.

The ascent is torture: long and drawn-out,
A ruthless test all nerves must pass.
15 But now we crest the peak and shout,
As one expectant, eager mass.

Excitement bursts its banks and floods
Our wild minds as now we fall.
Wind strikes faces, hair and hoods,
20 We howl out like banshees, all.

Goosebumps sprint up sweating skin,
With knuckles white as driven snow.
Through looping chaos; thrilling din,
We hold on tight and daren't let go.

25 And then — the end. We slow and stop
Where we began, but we're not the same.
Blood still racing as out we hop,
Our hearts now stallions that can't be tamed.

1. Which of the following is an example of personification?
    A "the queue snakes slowly"   B "Push out of mind"   C "Steel arms give a chill embrace"

2. "Our hearts now stallions that can't be tamed" (line 28). What technique is used here?
    A Simile   B Metaphor   C Personification

3. Which of the following is an example of a simile?
    A "Blood still racing"   B "white as driven snow"   C "looping chaos; thrilling din"

4. "Goosebumps sprint up sweating skin" (line 21). What technique is used here?
    A Simile   B Metaphor   C Personification

5. Which of the following is an example of a metaphor?
    A "Like runners in a one-horse race" (line 8)
    B "As one expectant, eager mass" (line 16)
    C "Excitement bursts its banks" (line 17)

/ 5

Spotting and Understanding Devices

> Read the passage below, then answer the questions that follow.

Shimmering with lights and bedecked with baubles, Christmas trees still bring a gasp of delight when they appear in homes around the world each December. But where did this festive icon originate? Many people believe that the tradition was established in Germany, where there are records from the sixteenth century of people bringing decorated trees inside.

5   Certainly, it was Queen Charlotte, the German wife of King George III, who introduced Christmas trees to England. In 1800, she installed a tree in the Queen's Lodge in Windsor, and adorned it with candles that filled the room with merrily dancing light.

One thing is for sure: the custom didn't come from thin air. Many ancient civilisations, including the Egyptians, are known to have decorated their homes and places of worship with

10   the boughs of evergreen trees at each winter solstice (the shortest day of the year). In this way, they marked the approaching return of life, like the dawning of hope, to their farms and fields.

The first artificial trees were created in the 1880s, and have increased in popularity ever since. At over 70 m high, and made of scrap metal and wood, an artificial tree in Sri Lanka currently holds the record for the tallest artificial tree in the world.

> Draw lines to connect each phrase from the text to the correct technique.

You will have one answer option left over.

1. "bedecked with baubles" (line 1)   Rhetorical question

2. "where did this festive icon originate?" (lines 2-3)   Onomatopoeia

                                                          Simile
3. "didn't come from thin air" (line 8)
                                                          Idiom
4. "return of life, like the dawning of hope" (line 11)   Alliteration

> Write down an example from the text of the following:

5.   personification   _____

6.   an abbreviation   _____

7.   a synonym of 'placed'   _____

8.   a synonym of 'man-made'   _____

9.   an antonym of 'displeasure'   _____

10. an antonym of 'reduced'   _____

/ 10

Section Two — Writers' Techniques

Spotting and Understanding Devices

Read the poem below, then answer the questions that follow.
Underline the correct option for each question.

I love this city with its shifting views,
Its winding, cobbled lanes and alleys
Where eager tourists, cameras poised
Flow like water in river valleys.

5   I love this city with its lively tune,
The rhythmic pulse of tram and car
That overlays the throb of voices,
That sounds both near at hand and far.

I love this city with its countless scents,
10 The salty air with its tang of sun-cream,
The tempting waft of fresh-cooked fish,
As carefree sunlight makes scales gleam.

I love this city for its people, my tribe,
For their familiar greetings as I stroll
15 Around the streets or along the old pier,
Feeling like a cog that's part of the whole.

It may not be Rio or Rouen or Rome*,
But I love this wonderful city, my home.

*Rio, Rouen, Rome — *large cities*
in Brazil, France and Italy

1.   The speaker says the tourists "Flow like water in river valleys" (line 4).
     What impression does this give you of the tourists?

     A They move downhill.   B They follow the same path.   C They move at random.

2.   The speaker describes the city's "lively tune" (line 5). This suggests that the city is:

     A painfully noisy.   B famous for music.   C stressful to be in.   D a fun place.

3.   The speaker describes "salty air", the "tang of sun-cream" and "fresh-cooked-fish" (lines 9-11).
     What effect does this description have on the reader?

     A It makes them hungry.   B It overwhelms them.   C It helps them imagine the smell.

4.   The speaker describes "Feeling like a cog that's part of the whole" (line 16).
     This suggests that they feel:

     A insignificant.   B integral.   C overworked.   D esteemed.

5.   Why does the speaker say "It may not be Rio or Rouen or Rome" (line 17)?

     A To show that their city might seem less exciting than other places.
     B To make the reader want to visit these other places.
     C To show that their city is the most impressive place they know.

/ 5

Spotting and Understanding Devices

Read the passage below, then answer the questions that follow.

In the corner of the playground, Ivy shoved her hands deeper into her pockets and stared fixedly at the scuffed toes of her school shoes. Sometimes, if she concentrated hard enough, she could make herself believe she was somewhere else — a deserted beach, a sunlit forest glade — anywhere. All around her rang the shrill shrieks and whoops of other children, but
5   Ivy stood adrift. She was a craggy, uninhabitable island in a shifting, swirling sea.

A group of boys eddied haphazardly past her: bobbing, spinning and completely oblivious to her presence. How must it feel to be part of something, she wondered. To be as fundamental to each others' existence as the planets in a solar system, or the bees in a hive.

"Hello," a quiet voice broke into her thoughts. She looked up, instinctively drawing back
10   her head like a tortoise. In front of her stood a boy she'd noticed standing in the opposite corner of the playground, staring fixedly at his own shoes. He tried out a smile that limped across his face, then slumped, exhausted. He cleared his throat and spoke again, the words coming out in a rush, "I've got a new microscope. D'you want to come and see it after school?"

Ivy swallowed, then slowly nodded. Perhaps she could be part of something after all.

Underline the word from the brackets that best completes each sentence.

1.   In line 5, Ivy feels _____ . **(resentful   nervous   isolated)**

2.   In line 6, the boys are described like _____ . **(driftwood   islands   clouds)**

3.   Lines 7-8 suggest that belonging to a group is _____ . **(amusing   rare   natural)**

Underline the correct option for each question.

4.   Why do you think Ivy pulls back her head "like a tortoise" (line 10)?
     A She doesn't like the boy.   **B** She can't see the boy clearly.   **C** She feels vulnerable.

5.   The boy's smile "limped across his face, then slumped, exhausted" (lines 11-12).
     This suggests that he:
     A smiles too often.   **B** is not usually sociable.   **C** is extremely tired.

6.   What do the noises in line 4 suggest about the playground's atmosphere?
     A It is frightening.   **B** It is joyful.   **C** It is tense.

/ 6

Assessment Test 1

The rest of the book contains seven assessment tests, which get progressively harder.

Allow 28 minutes to do each test and work as quickly and as carefully as you can.

If you want to attempt each test more than once, you will need to print
multiple-choice answer sheets for these questions from our website —
go to cgpbooks.co.uk/11plus/answer-sheets or scan the QR code on the right. If you'd
prefer to answer the questions on the page, just follow the instructions in the question.

Answer Sheets

Read this passage carefully and answer the questions that follow.

Escaped Critters Lead Locals on a Meery Dance

Residents of Little Duffing were treated to an intriguing spectacle last week as dozens of meerkats swarmed the town centre. The animals, which had made an audacious bid for freedom from a nearby safari park, were witnessed scampering into shops on Swan Street, tunnelling through compost heaps in the garden centre and wreaking havoc under the stalls in the indoor market before being captured.

5   "I only leant my ladder against the wall of the enclosure for a minute while I refilled their food," red-faced keeper Lenny Scritch told journalists, "and when I turned round all I could see was a river of tawny fur pouring out of the main entrance to the zoo. I can't believe they outwitted me."

Local workers and passersby attempted to ensnare the furry mischief-makers by herding them towards the pond in Mill Lane Park, but realised they were barking up the wrong tree when the pack
10   gleefully scurried over a floating log to the far side. They were eventually captured by wildlife expert Kitty Chao, who, having resided in southern Africa, is familiar with their habits and dietary requirements.

"I collected caterpillars, grubs, bits of melon," Ms Chao explained, "and wood chips for them to burrow into. No meerkat could resist.   Before long, I had them safely detained and ready to go home."

This playful posse are not alone in seeking a new life outside captivity: last year alone saw several
15   breakouts from the park, and Snappy the turtle remains at large.

Answer these questions about the text that you've just read.
Circle the letter of the correct answer.

1.   How did the meerkats escape from their enclosure?

   A   They went out of the door after the keeper left it open.
   B   They tricked their keeper by distracting him with food.
   C   They tunnelled under the wall of the enclosure.
   D   They climbed over the wall of their enclosure.
   E   They swam out of the enclosure along a stream.

2.   Which of these words best describes how Lenny Scritch feels?

   A   Furious
   B   Embarrassed
   C   Proud
   D   Puzzled
   E   Anxious

/ 2

Carry on to the next question → →

3. Which of the following is not mentioned as a place the meerkats visited?

    A A park
    B A wood
    C A pond
    D A store
    E A market

4. Local residents "realised they were barking up the wrong tree" (line 9).
    This means that they were:

    A looking in the wrong place.
    B using dogs to find the meerkats.
    C mistaken in thinking meerkats could not climb.
    D confused about how the meerkats got away.
    E taking the wrong approach.

5. Which of the following is not mentioned in the text?

    A Where the meerkats escaped from
    B What meerkats like to eat
    C Whether meerkats can dig
    D How large meerkats' burrows are
    E What colour meerkats are

6. According to the passage, how did Kitty Chao learn about meerkats?

    A She had studied them at university.
    B She had lived in an area where they are native.
    C She had worked in a safari park.
    D She had asked the keeper for advice.
    E She had run a meerkat-themed restaurant.

7. According to the passage, which of the following statements is true?

    A The meerkats attacked local residents in Little Duffing.
    B The safari park is home to fewer than twenty meerkats.
    C More animals have escaped this year than in previous years.
    D Not all of the animals that have escaped have been recaptured.
    E The same keeper is responsible for letting other animals escape.

8. Where would you be most likely to find this text?

    A A newspaper
    B An encyclopedia
    C An autobiography
    D A travel brochure
    E A recipe book

/ 6

Answer these questions about the way words and phrases are used in the passage.

9. Which of these words is closest in meaning to "audacious" (line 2)?

   A Thoughtless
   B Daring
   C Dangerous
   D Cunning
   E Foolhardy

10. Which of these words is closest in meaning to "havoc" (line 4)?

    A Panic
    B Clutter
    C Wreckage
    D Trouble
    E Chaos

11. Which word could most accurately replace "ensnare" (line 8)?

    A Deter
    B Assist
    C Corner
    D Shield
    E Save

12. What part of speech is "food" (line 5)?

    A Collective noun
    B Proper noun
    C Abstract noun
    D Pronoun
    E Common noun

13. "This playful posse are not alone" (line 14).
    This is an example of:

    A a metaphor.
    B irony.
    C alliteration.
    D a simile.
    E onomatopoeia.

14. What type of words are these?

    intriguing   local   dietary   ready

    A Adverbs
    B Verbs
    C Prepositions
    D Adjectives
    E Pronouns

/ 6

Carry on to the next question → →

26

> Read this passage carefully and answer the questions that follow.

Sakura's Garden

   Perched on the edge of her seat at the back of the school bus, Sakura clutched her miniature garden with trembling fingers, doing her best to brace it against each bump and jolt. All around her, other containers filled with greenery and flowers rested carelessly on pupils' laps or lay beneath seats, as disregarded as cast-off socks. Nathan Baker mimed a wrestling move, and in doing so
5 gestured flamboyantly with his garden, sending fragments of grit and soil rattling down the aisle.

   The bus drew up at the Birch Street stop, and Sakura took the opportunity to place her garden gingerly on her lap and ensure that nothing had become disordered. She ran a finger lightly over the feathery ferns that clustered around the tiny rockery; the blue glass pebbles, as brightly polished as jewels, that formed a winding stream; the array of minute wildflowers that studded the moss like
10 stars in a velvet sky. She let out a deep breath: her garden was exquisite, and nobody else's could come close to rivalling it.

   Just then, the Birch Street pupils clambered onto the bus. Sally Chalke trailed behind as usual, her shirt buttons in the wrong holes and her once-white socks bunched and rumpled around her ankles. Sakura suddenly stiffened. Sally's grubby fingers were clamped around a terracotta tray that
15 contained a minuscule wonderland. Delicate bridges spanned gravel paths that wound in and out between groves of tiny trees, while cascades of miniature scented flowers spilled over rocky banks. Sakura scrutinised her own garden, but the glass pebbles now appeared dingy and lacklustre.

> Answer these questions about the text that you've just read.
> Circle the letter of the correct answer.

15. Why are Sakura's fingers "trembling" (line 2)?

   A She is frightened of travelling to school.
   B She is being shaken by the movement of the bus.
   C She is worried that her miniature garden will be ruined.
   D She is angry that the bus driver is driving carelessly.
   E She is tired after staying up late to finish her miniature garden.

16. Nathan Baker "gestured flamboyantly with his garden" (line 5).
    What does this suggest about him?

   A He wants to show his miniature garden off to other pupils.
   B He doesn't take good care of his miniature garden.
   C He does not perform the wrestling move very skilfully.
   D He didn't put much effort into his miniature garden.
   E He wants to distract other pupils from Sakura's miniature garden.

/ 2

17. Why does Sakura put her miniature garden down when the bus stops?

    A   She is preparing to get off the bus.
    B   She wants to give her hands a rest from holding it.
    C   She thinks it will be safer on her lap.
    D   She wants to look at it carefully.
    E   She is worried about getting soil on her hands.

18. Which of the following things does Sakura's miniature garden not contain?

    A   Tiny feathers
    B   A pretend river
    C   Pieces of blue glass
    D   Small chunks of rock
    E   Several types of plant

19. Why does Sakura "let out a deep breath" (line 10)?

    A   She is trying to control her emotions.
    B   She is relieved that her miniature garden is undamaged.
    C   She is worried about the rest of the journey.
    D   She is annoyed by other pupils' carelessness.
    E   She is trying to focus on improving her miniature garden.

20. "nobody else's could come close to rivalling it" (lines 10-11).
    This tells you that Sakura thinks her miniature garden is:

    A   of equal quality to the other gardens.
    B   completely flawless.
    C   going to win a competition.
    D   the best one on the bus.
    E   envied by the other pupils.

21. Which of the following statements about Sally is false?

    A   Her shirt is fastened incorrectly.
    B   Her socks are not new.
    C   Her shirt is stained.
    D   Her hands are dirty.
    E   Her socks are loose.

22. Which of the following best describes Sakura's feelings after she sees Sally's miniature garden?

    A   Outraged
    B   Disbelieving
    C   Impressed
    D   Disheartened
    E   Enchanted

/ 6

Answer these questions about the way words and phrases are used in the passage.

23. Which word could most accurately replace "brace" (line 2)?

    A Catch
    B Assemble
    C Influence
    D Steady
    E Endure

24. Which word could most accurately replace "gingerly" (line 7)?

    A Apprehensively
    B Cautiously
    C Discreetly
    D Suspiciously
    E Reluctantly

25. Which of these words is closest in meaning to "scrutinised" (line 17)?

    A Inspected
    B Glimpsed
    C Caressed
    D Compared
    E Visualised

26. "ensure that nothing had become disordered" (line 7). Which word in this sentence is an adjective?

    A ensure
    B nothing
    C had
    D become
    E disordered

27. What technique is used in the phrase
"sending fragments of grit and soil whizzing down the aisle" (line 5)?

    A Personification
    B Metaphor
    C Alliteration
    D Simile
    E Onomatopoeia

28. The miniature gardens are "as disregarded as cast-off socks" (line 4). What is this an example of?

    A Irony
    B A simile
    C An analogy
    D Personification
    E A metaphor

/ 6

Total / 28

End of Test

Assessment Test 2

Allow 28 minutes to do this test and work as quickly and as carefully as you can.

You can print **multiple-choice answer sheets** for these questions from our website — go to cgpbooks.co.uk/11plus/answer-sheets or scan the QR code on the right. If you'd prefer to answer the questions on the page, just follow the instructions in the question.

Answer Sheets

> Read this passage carefully and answer the questions that follow.

Yellowstone

Renowned for its diverse landforms and abundant wildlife, Yellowstone National Park is a gold mine of mesmerising natural features. Spanning an overall area just shy of 9000 km^2, approximately 96% of the park is located in the state of Wyoming, with the rest spilling into Montana and Idaho. Yellowstone was the first national park in the United States, acquiring this title in 1872. It is widely (though not universally)
5   regarded as the world's first national park.

Lying beneath Yellowstone's striking scenery is a dormant supervolcano. Historically, this slumbering giant has violently erupted at roughly 700 000 year intervals. While a severe eruption is improbable in our lifetime, scientists still monitor the volcano continuously for any signs of activity.

Yellowstone's volcanic landscape is home to pools of hot water known as hot springs. In some of
10   these springs, concentric circles in vibrant hues spread outwards from the centre. These rainbow rings are caused by different types of microorganism that have adapted to thrive in hot water. However, they are so bizarre that observers may be forgiven for assuming they are artificial or even supernatural in origin.

Yellowstone is also dotted with geysers — a rare type of water feature that extends deep underground. The water within geysers is heated by magma below, and as the temperature of the water
15   climbs, the pressure also soars. Eventually, the superheated water turns into steam and shoots into the air in a captivating display. Yellowstone boasts the highest concentration of active geysers in the world, with the most famous of these being *Old Faithful*.

> Answer these questions about the text that you've just read.
> Circle the letter of the correct answer.

1. Which statement about Yellowstone National Park is false?

    A It is well known for its natural landmarks.
    B It covers more than 9000 km^2.
    C It is the oldest national park in the United States.
    D It was founded in the late 19th century.
    E It is mostly within Wyoming.

2. According to the text, which of the following statements is true?

    A Everyone agrees that Yellowstone was the first national park in the world.
    B Everyone agrees that Yellowstone was not the first national park in the world.
    C Not everyone agrees that Yellowstone was the first national park in the world.
    D Only a few people believe that Yellowstone was the first national park in the world.
    E People used to believe that Yellowstone was the first national park in the world.

/ 2

Carry on to the next question → →

3. "scientists still monitor the volcano continuously for any signs of activity" (line 8).
    What does this phrase mean?

    A Scientists only monitor the volcano when they are told to.
    B Scientists rarely monitor the volcano.
    C Scientists are always monitoring the volcano.
    D Scientists only monitor the volcano remotely.
    E Scientists only monitor the volcano when there are signs of volcanic activity.

4. Which of the following facts about the Yellowstone volcano is not mentioned in the text?

    A How likely it is that it will erupt soon
    B How many years ago it last erupted
    C How often catastrophic eruptions happen
    D How active it currently is
    E Where it is situated

5. The text mentions "concentric circles in vibrant hues" (line 10). What does this mean?

    A Loops of vivid colours
    B Spheres of fossilised stones
    C Rings of bright flowers
    D Bands of abstract patterns
    E Circles of edible mushrooms

6. According to the text, what could you find in some hot springs?

    A Pieces of microplastic
    B Tiny living things
    C A variety of plants
    D Lots of minerals
    E Small crystals

7. According to the text, watching a geyser erupt is:

    A nerve-racking.
    B underwhelming.
    C gripping.
    D haunting.
    E tiresome.

8. According to the text, which of the following facts about geysers is false?

    A The water in geysers reaches a very high temperature.
    B *Old Faithful* is a well-known geyser.
    C Erupting geysers eject steam at high speeds.
    D Geysers are a widespread geographical feature.
    E The water in geysers reaches a very high pressure.

/ 6

Answer these questions about the way words and phrases are used in the passage.

9. The word "diverse" (line 1) could most accurately be replaced by:

   A distinctive.
   B conflicting.
   C varied.
   D changeable.
   E inspiring.

10. Which of these words is closest in meaning to "thrive" (line 11)?

    A Adjust
    B Flourish
    C Dissolve
    D Survive
    E Combine

11. Which of these words is closest in meaning to "observers" (line 12)?

    A Passersby
    B Visitors
    C Inspectors
    D Customers
    E Spectators

12. "Yellowstone National Park is a gold mine" (line 1).
    Which technique is used here?

    A An abbreviation
    B Personification
    C A simile
    D Irony
    E A metaphor

13. "the rest spilling into Montana and Idaho" (line 3).
    Which word in this sentence is a preposition?

    A the
    B rest
    C spilling
    D into
    E and

14. What technique is used in the phrase "Lying beneath Yellowstone's striking scenery" (line 6)?

    A Onomatopoeia
    B Alliteration
    C Simile
    D Irony
    E Analogy

/ 6

Carry on to the next question → →

> Read this passage carefully and answer the questions that follow.

An abridged extract from 'Savi and the Memory Keeper'

Shajarpur has a happy climate — just right in the summer, just right in the winter, just right in the monsoon*, and so *gloriously* right in the spring. No wonder Shajarpurians feel like they're Goldilocks with the just-right bowl of porridge.

The result? People constantly boasting about the weather. When we got off the flight, rumpled,
5   tired, and grumbly (me still metaphorically kicking and screaming), a woman at the gate thrust a rose at us and beamed, "Welcome to Shajarpur, the city with the best climate in the world!" The rose was pearly fresh, as if just plucked from a Mughal* garden.

* * *

So here we were in Shajarpur. A city where —

Happiness was a low electricity bill. It was a matter of pride that nobody needed to own an air
10 conditioner. Fans, sure! To be turned on in the peak of May for exactly 4.6 days. Or to drive away the occasional fly that made its way into a room.

Open cafes spilled out onto terraces and tree-lined roadsides. Gardens burst with blossoms and citizens picnicked there without hardworking *maalis** asking them to stay off the grass. There were sparkling lakes where birdwatchers would go birdwatching, frog-watchers would go frog-watching,
15 and insect-watchers would go insect-watching.

Doctors were thankfully miserable because of their minuscule incomes — people rarely fell sick here, but bureaucrats were thrilled as they had to do little beyond basic maintenance here and there. It was a good life.

School lessons were also a little bit different from other cities. Yes, they learned about climate
20 change, but it was like something that happened to other people, other species, and other places. After all, their climate was perfect.

The newspaper weather report section was called "The Happiness Report." *Not* kidding.

No wonder people had begun to pour in from every part of India and the world to make Shajarpur their new home. Like us.

by Bijal Vachharajani

*monsoon — *a season of heavy rain in hot countries*
*Mughal — *an empire that ruled most of India between the 16th and 18th centuries*
*maalis — *gardeners*

> Answer these questions about the text that you've just read.
> Circle the letter of the correct answer.

15. Which of the following best describes how people from Shajarpur talk about the weather?

   A They are always exaggerating how good it is.
   B They rarely talk about it.
   C They don't talk about it when it is bad.
   D They are always talking about how good it is.
   E They only talk about it when it is good.

16. Which of these best describes the narrator when they arrive in Shajarpur?

   A Hungry and unwell
   B Furious and aggressive
   C Weary and untidy
   D Anxious and confused
   E Upset and overheated

/ 2

17. Why do you think the narrator specifies the exact length of time that fans are used for each year?

   A   To show off how detailed their knowledge is
   B   To boast about how brief a time it is
   C   To mock the people of Shajarpur for their pride
   D   To hint that they think fans should be used more
   E   To reveal how excited they are to use a fan

18. Which of the following is given in the text as a reason for using fans?

   A   To save money
   B   To use less energy
   C   To benefit people's health
   D   To improve air quality
   E   To ward off insects

19. Why are doctors in Shajarpur unhappy?

   A   Because they are often ill
   B   Because they do not earn very much money
   C   Because they are always stressed
   D   Because they do not enjoy their jobs
   E   Because other people don't work as hard as them

20. Which of the following isn't mentioned in the text?

   A   Places to eat with outdoor seating
   B   People watching birds by lakes
   C   Gardens with flowers
   D   Streets lined with trees
   E   Gardeners having picnics

21. Which of the following statements about Shajarpur is false?

   A   Climate change is taught in Shajarpur's schools.
   B   People don't need air conditioning in Shajarpur.
   C   The weather in Shajarpur is at its best during summer.
   D   Shajarpur experiences a rainy season.
   E   "The Happiness Report" informs readers about the weather in Shajarpur.

22. Which of the following statements is true?

   A   The narrator is originally from Shajarpur.
   B   The narrator is surprised Shajarpur is popular.
   C   The narrator is moving to Shajarpur.
   D   The narrator is in Shajarpur alone.
   E   The narrator is visiting Shajarpur on holiday.

/ 6

> Answer these questions about the way words and phrases are used in the passage.

23. What does the word "metaphorically" (line 5) mean?

   A Assertively
   B Literally
   C Accidentally
   D Figuratively
   E Silently

24. The word "beamed" (line 6) could most accurately be replaced by:

   A announced.
   B grinned.
   C cheered.
   D shouted.
   E grimaced.

25. What does the word "thrilled" (line 17) mean?

   A Relieved
   B Delighted
   C Fortunate
   D Impressed
   E Relaxed

26. What type of word is "pride" (line 9)?

   A Abstract noun
   B Concrete noun
   C Collective noun
   D Proper noun
   E Pronoun

27. "Shajarpur has a happy climate" (line 1). Which technique is used here?

   A A metaphor
   B Personification
   C Irony
   D An idiom
   E A simile

28. What technique is used in the phrase "Gardens burst with blossoms" (line 12)?

   A Cliché
   B Simile
   C Personification
   D Onomatopoeia
   E Alliteration

/ 6

Total | / 28

End of Test

Assessment Test 3

Allow 28 minutes to do this test and work as quickly and as carefully as you can.

You can print **multiple-choice answer sheets** for these questions from our website — go to cgpbooks.co.uk/11plus/answer-sheets or scan the QR code on the right. If you'd prefer to answer the questions on the page, just follow the instructions in the question.

Answer Sheets

> Read this passage carefully and answer the questions that follow.

Your Next Big Adventure

If spectacular scenery, riveting races and dazzling dance displays make your heart race, the Lake Turkana Cultural Festival might just be the holiday destination of your dreams. Centred around the town of Loiyangalani on the tranquil shore of Lake Turkana, the festival is a celebration of the diverse communities living in and around the Marsabit region of northern
5 Kenya in east Africa. With more than 15 years of success under its belt, the festival now captivates more than 50 000 visitors each year over three days.

The remarkable event includes something for everyone. If you're a culture vulture, you'll be spoilt for choice: spend the day enjoying an array of traditional regional music, dance and costumes, then refuel with some delectable local dishes. No trip to the Marsabit region would be
10 complete without marvelling at the skill of the local beadworkers. Ushanga (from the Swahili for 'beads') is the art of threading vibrant beads onto clothing, jewellery and accessories to enhance their beauty. If sport is more your thing, perhaps watching the boat races on Lake Turkana or a 14-kilometre foot race through the nearby hills will appeal.

With so much bustle and excitement going on around you, it would be easy to overlook the
15 more serious side of the festival. Participants from at least ten ethnic groups attend, each with their own customs and beliefs, so the event is an important opportunity to promote cooperation and kinship. Now who wouldn't want to be a part of that?

> Answer these questions about the text that you've just read.
> Circle the letter of the correct answer.

1. What does the phrase "make your heart race" (line 1) suggest about the features mentioned?

   A They may be frightening.
   B They may surprise you.
   C They may make you exert yourself.
   D They may appeal to you.
   E They may be rewarding.

2. Which of the following places is not mentioned in the text?

   A The town where much of the festival takes place
   B The region where the festival occurs
   C The body of water where some events happen
   D The country where the festival is located
   E The place where most visitors come from

/ 2

3. Which of these statements about the festival is true?

   A It lasts for less than a week.
   B It has been running for less than a decade.
   C It happens only every other year.
   D It attracts half a million visitors each time.
   E It takes place near the sea.

4. Which of the following best describes the author's opinion of the festival?

   A Relaxing and peaceful
   B Confusing and noisy
   C Stimulating and varied
   D Lively and chaotic
   E Friendly and welcoming

5. What do you think the phrase "culture vulture" (line 7) means?

   A Someone who sets trends in fashion
   B Someone who is interested in the arts
   C Someone who enjoys meeting new people
   D Someone who is highly educated
   E Someone who has travelled to many countries

6. Which of the following activities does the text not mention visitors participating in?

   A Watching people crafting
   B Seeing a running contest
   C Eating local food
   D Swimming in the lake
   E Listening to music

7. Which of the following facts about "Ushanga" (line 10) is not given in the passage?

   A What language the word comes from
   B Why people practise the art
   C How the beads are attached
   D What types of objects are decorated
   E Where the art form originated

8. Where would you be most likely to find this text?

   A An encyclopedia
   B A travel brochure
   C A book of letters
   D An autobiography
   E An atlas

/ 6

Answer these questions about the way words and phrases are used in the passage.

9. Which of these words is closest in meaning to "riveting" (line 1)?

   A Winning
   B Gripping
   C Striking
   D Pleasing
   E Looming

10. Which of these words could most accurately replace "promote" (line 16)?

   A Further
   B Praise
   C Confirm
   D Justify
   E Strain

11. "15 years of success under its belt" (line 5). What technique is used here?

   A Idiom
   B Irony
   C Alliteration
   D Simile
   E Onomatopoeia

12. "cooperation and kinship" (line 17) is an example of what technique?

   A Simile
   B Personification
   C Onomatopoeia
   D Alliteration
   E Abbreviation

13. What type of word is "onto" (line 11)?

   A Verb
   B Preposition
   C Adjective
   D Adverb
   E Noun

14. "so much bustle and excitement going on around you" (line 14).
    Which of these words is a pronoun?

   A so
   B bustle
   C on
   D around
   E you

/ 6

Carry on to the next question → →

> Read this passage carefully and answer the questions that follow.

Lost in Translation

It was late in the evening, and everyone else in the linguistics department had left their offices many hours earlier. As though reluctant for anyone to see it in this vulnerable state, the university building had an unfriendly air. But on the second floor, a warm, yellow light outlined the edge of a door that had a plaque reading "Dr Imani Kirunda".

5   Several months ago, the government had sent a classified email to the head of Imani's department. A satellite orbiting Earth had intercepted a message from the other side of the galaxy. After failing to decipher it themselves, the government had concluded that it was a job for one of the most esteemed groups of language researchers in the country. Imani and her colleagues had dropped everything to concentrate on this thrilling task — who wouldn't want to be one of the first people to

10 translate an alien message?

However, as the weeks slipped by and progress was non-existent, working on it became more and more of a chore. Imani was the only one of the original team who remained intrigued. She'd always had an aptitude for languages: she was fluent in nine, and her extensive knowledge meant she could normally figure out at least a rough translation of anything else. This language, however, was

15 like nothing she'd ever encountered, and it fascinated her. She often stayed late trying to translate it, and tonight was one of those occasions.

On the glowing screen in her office, the symbols of the message sat smugly, obstinately defying comprehension. She gazed at them, willing them to reveal their meanings. The marks looked... half-finished, as though parts of them were missing. *What if...?* She grabbed two of the many paper

20 copies strewn around her, overlaid them back-to-back, and held them up to the light. It was like pieces of a puzzle coming together. Immediately she could see patterns in the symbols, repeated phrases and structure that had been absent before now. A triumphant smile washed across her face as she realised that this was the breakthrough they'd all been waiting for.

> Answer these questions about the text that you've just read.
> Circle the letter of the correct answer.

15. Which of these statements is false?

    A Imani works on the second floor.
    B Imani has her own office.
    C Imani works at a university.
    D Imani runs the department.
    E Imani speaks several languages.

16. Which of these words best describes the email that was sent to the linguistics department?

    A Long
    B Urgent
    C Boring
    D Scheduled
    E Secret

/ 2

17. What does the department do when they receive the email from the government?

    A   They decide to ignore it for a few months.
    B   They stop their current work to focus on the message.
    C   They start to work on the message alongside their usual tasks.
    D   They reply to the email asking for more information.
    E   They ask Imani to work on the message alone.

18. Imani's colleagues start to view working on the message as
    "more and more of a chore" (lines 11-12). This suggests that:

    A   they don't care what it says anymore.
    B   they are regretting their earlier work on it.
    C   they think translating it is impossible.
    D   they are starting to find it boring.
    E   they have been working on it too much.

19. Why is Imani so interested in the message?

    A   Because she knows it is about her.
    B   Because she has been asked to work on it.
    C   Because she hasn't come across a similar language.
    D   Because she is fluent in the language used.
    E   Because she wants to prove people wrong.

20. Why does Imani try overlapping copies of the message?

    A   She thinks the symbols look incomplete.
    B   She dreamed the idea the night before.
    C   She does it by accident.
    D   She is in the process of tidying them away.
    E   She loses focus on the screen and they blur together.

21. Which of the following facts is given in the passage?

    A   Imani's age
    B   Imani's surname
    C   What Imani is wearing
    D   The name of one of Imani's colleagues
    E   The country Imani is in

22. According to the text, how does Imani feel when she works out how to interpret the language?

    A   Tired
    B   Proud
    C   Startled
    D   Amazed
    E   Amused

    / 6

Answer these questions about the way words and phrases are used in the passage.

23. The linguistics department is "esteemed" (line 8). This means the department is:

    A well-respected.
    B exclusive.
    C famous.
    D dependable.
    E organised.

24. Which of these is closest in meaning to the word "aptitude" (line 13)?

    A Passion
    B Soft spot
    C Thirst
    D Curiosity
    E Talent

25. Which of these words is closest in meaning to "extensive" (line 13)?

    A Impressive
    B Convenient
    C Natural
    D Large
    E Expert

26. Which of these words could most accurately replace "obstinately" (line 17)?

    A Perfectly
    B Brightly
    C Teasingly
    D Neatly
    E Stubbornly

27. "the symbols of the message sat smugly" (line 17). This is an example of:

    A personification.
    B a simile.
    C onomatopoeia.
    D a cliché.
    E a rhetorical question.

28. What type of word is "sent" (line 5)?

    A Proper noun
    B Adjective
    C Adverb
    D Verb
    E Common noun

/ 6

Total   / 28

End of Test

Assessment Test 4

Allow 28 minutes to do this test and work as quickly and as carefully as you can.

You can print **multiple-choice answer sheets** for these questions from our website —
go to cgpbooks.co.uk/11plus/answer-sheets or scan the QR code on the right. If you'd
prefer to answer the questions on the page, just follow the instructions in the question.

> Read this passage carefully and answer the questions that follow.

The Legend of Doxey Pool

On a hot summer's day, the prospect of cooling off with an al fresco* swim might seem appealing.
If you live in Staffordshire, however, you may want to exercise some caution in choosing your spot.
Doxey Pool, located on a rocky outcrop known as the Roaches in the south-western Peak District
National Park, has a somewhat sinister reputation.

5   Despite being modest in size, some claim that the pool is bottomless: as evidence, they cite
the fact that, even during drought conditions, the water level never drops significantly. If that's not
enough to deter you, local legend maintains that the lake is home to a malevolent mermaid. Known
as Jenny Greenteeth or Wicked Jenny, her aim is to lure unwary passersby into the water, where
they meet their end.

10   One person who claimed to have seen the lake's supernatural inhabitant was a young local
woman named Florence Pettit. One morning in 1949, Florence ventured to the pool for a pre-lunch
dip before meeting a friend. As she was on the verge of entering the water, a huge being rose from
the depths until it stood over seven metres tall, with its feet resting on the surface of the water. The
creature, which appeared to be formed from water weed, glared and pointed a finger threateningly
15 at the terrified intruder, before sinking back into the depths.

     Whether this sighting was authentic or merely the consequence of imagination, deceit or an
excess of sun, the pool retains an eerie atmosphere and notoriety amongst uneasy locals.

*al fresco — *taking place outside*

> Answer these questions about the text that you've just read.
> Circle the letter of the correct answer.

1. Which of the following statements about the location of Doxey Pool is false?

    A It is in a rocky area.
    B It is in a National Park.
    C It is in the south-west of the UK.
    D It is in Staffordshire.
    E It is in an area called the Roaches.

2. Why do some people believe that Doxey Pool has no bottom?

    A It is never more than half full of water.
    B The water surface always stays at about the same height.
    C Nobody has ever managed to reach the bottom.
    D There has never been a drought in the area.
    E It is home to a very large creature.

/ 2

Carry on to the next question → →

3. According to the text, which of the following statements about Doxey Pool is true?

   A It is quite small.
   B The water has magical properties.
   C It's the only place in the area to swim.
   D It's in a busy area.
   E People are advised to avoid it.

4. According to the passage, what does the Doxey Pool mermaid try to do to her victims?

   A Scold them
   B Warn them
   C Repel them
   D Educate them
   E Drown them

5. According to the passage, which of the following statements best describes Jenny Greenteeth's appearance?

   A Slim with a long tail
   B Enormous and green
   C Tall and extremely thin
   D Delicate and made of flowers
   E Massive and scaly

6. Which of the following statements about Florence Pettit is false?

   A She intended to swim in Doxey Pool.
   B She lived quite close to Doxey Pool.
   C She was scared by her encounter with the mermaid.
   D She visited Doxey Pool with a friend.
   E She saw the mermaid before she got into the pool.

7. Which of the following is not given as a possible explanation for the sighting of the mermaid?

   A The sun made Florence hallucinate.
   B Florence lied about seeing the mermaid.
   C Florence saw a branch swathed in weeds.
   D The mermaid was real.
   E Florence dreamed up the mermaid.

8. According to the text, how do local people feel about Doxey Pool?

   A They enjoy the fame it brings.
   B They avoid it at all costs.
   C They like the peaceful atmosphere.
   D They are proud of the legends about it.
   E They view it with apprehension.

/ 6

Answer these questions about the way words and phrases are used in the passage.

9. Which of these words could most accurately replace "exercise" (line 2)?

    A Workout
    B Apply
    C Specify
    D Retain
    E Possess

10. Which of these words is closest in meaning to "deter" (line 7)?

    A Oppose
    B Entice
    C Frustrate
    D Counteract
    E Discourage

11. Which of these words is closest in meaning to "malevolent" (line 7)?

    A Mischievous
    B Ruthless
    C Grotesque
    D Evil
    E Brutal

12. What technique is used in the phrase "somewhat sinister" (line 4)?

    A Idiom
    B Cliché
    C Alliteration
    D Abbreviation
    E Personification

13. What type of word is "cite" (line 5)?

    A Noun
    B Verb
    C Adverb
    D Preposition
    E Conjunction

14. "it stood over seven metres tall" (line 13). Which word in this sentence is a pronoun?

    A it
    B stood
    C over
    D seven
    E metres

/ 6

Carry on to the next question → →

Assessment Test 4

> Read this passage carefully and answer the questions that follow.

Ambush

Flat on her stomach, with the sagging mattress above her restricting the available space, Krista shifted position again. However she arranged her limbs, her knees and elbows seemed to seek out the hardest areas of floorboard. Still, she reminded herself, sometimes it was necessary to suffer for your cause. Though not if you were Kurt, it seemed — glancing at her younger brother next to her,
5 she noticed that he'd fallen asleep again. A faint snore issued from his mouth and she elbowed him sharply: she wouldn't allow him to bungle this operation and let the burglar escape them once more.

Over the past week, a series of trinkets had gone missing from their home. Some, like their father's gold watch and the silver bracelet Krista's grandparents had given her for her birthday, were quite valuable. Others, including a cake fork, a screwdriver and a key for an unidentified lock,
10 were just plain bizarre. Kurt had a theory that the thief knew the location of a magnificent hidden treasure, and needed all the items to access it. Krista thought that seemed rather far-fetched: for a start, what possible function could the bracelet have in that scenario?

Krista surveyed the collection of objects that she and Kurt had arranged on the desk between the window and the door: a gleaming silver teaspoon rested artlessly against a pair of pliers, while a
15 necklace of sparkling beads was draped enticingly over the top. Beside her, Kurt shuffled restlessly and sighed; she scowled and gave him a cautionary nudge, raising a finger to her lips.

Becoming aware of a noise from somewhere in the room, they both tensed simultaneously. Krista inched forward, craning her neck. There was a sudden surge of ebony and a loud flapping, like someone violently shaking out an umbrella, and they both jerked backwards. On the desk, a large,
20 ash-flecked jackdaw glanced around, plucked the pliers from the pile, swooped down to the fireplace and vanished, leaving no trace but a sooty footprint on the desk.

> Answer these questions about the text that you've just read.
> Circle the letter of the correct answer.

15. Krista thinks that "sometimes it was necessary to suffer for your cause" (lines 3-4).
    What do you think this means?

    A Pursuing your goals might cause difficulties for other people.
    B You might be injured if you try to catch a criminal yourself.
    C If you plan something carefully enough, you cannot fail.
    D You may need to experience hardship to achieve your aims.
    E Defending your principles to other people can be difficult.

16. Which of the following items was not stolen?

    A Some cutlery
    B A padlock
    C Some jewellery
    D A timepiece
    E Some tools

/ 2

17. Why do you think Krista and Kurt chose the objects they placed on the desk?

    A They would all be useful for finding hidden treasure.
    B They are valuable, so a thief would be drawn to them.
    C They are easy to replace, so it doesn't matter if they are stolen.
    D They are distinctive, so it would be easy to spot the thief using them.
    E They are similar to the items that have already gone missing.

18. Which of the following best describes Krista's view of Kurt's theory?

    A It is improbable because they would have heard about the treasure.
    B It is fanciful because Kurt has a very vivid imagination.
    C It is unconvincing because the stolen objects are not useful.
    D It is implausible, but there is no reason that it cannot be true.
    E It is unlikely because the thief left other, more valuable items behind.

19. Why does Krista scowl at Kurt?

    A She is worried that he will reveal their presence.
    B She wants him to wake up before the thief arrives.
    C She wishes he had found a different hiding place.
    D She is concerned that he will tell someone their plan.
    E She is annoyed that he spotted the thief before she did.

20. "Krista inched forward, craning her neck" (line 18).
    Why do you think she does this?

    A She is getting ready to jump out.
    B She wants to make herself look bigger.
    C She is attempting to get a better view.
    D She wants to stop Kurt from moving.
    E She is trying to get more comfortable.

21. How does the thief get in and out of the room?

    A It comes in through the window and goes out through the chimney.
    B It comes in through the chimney and goes out through the door.
    C It comes in through the door and goes out through the chimney.
    D It comes in through the door and goes out through a hidden opening.
    E It comes in through the chimney and goes out through the chimney.

22. Which of the following statements is false?

    A This is Krista and Kurt's first attempt to catch the thief.
    B Kurt and Krista hear the thief entering at the same time.
    C Krista is older than Kurt.
    D Krista does not know why the thief has stolen certain items.
    E Krista and Kurt are hiding in a bedroom.

/ 6

Answer these questions about the way words and phrases are used in the passage.

23. Which of these words is closest in meaning to "bungle" (line 6)?

    A   Neglect
    B   Spoil
    C   Waste
    D   Control
    E   Dishonour

24. Which of these words is closest in meaning to "artlessly" (line 14)?

    A   Unattractively
    B   Cleverly
    C   Beautifully
    D   Conspicuously
    E   Naturally

25. Which of these words is closest in meaning to "cautionary" (line 16)?

    A   Warning
    B   Savage
    C   Irritated
    D   Surly
    E   Cheeky

26. Krista's "knees and elbows seemed to seek out the hardest areas of floorboard" (lines 2-3).
    What technique is used here?

    A   Irony
    B   Simile
    C   Personification
    D   Onomatopoeia
    E   Analogy

27. "a loud flapping, like someone violently shaking out an umbrella" (lines 18-19). This is an example of:

    A   a simile.
    B   a metaphor.
    C   alliteration.
    D   a cliché.
    E   personification.

28. What part of speech is "from" (line 5)?

    A   Noun
    B   Pronoun
    C   Preposition
    D   Adjective
    E   Adverb

/ 6

Total   / 28

End of Test

Assessment Test 5

Allow 28 minutes to do this test and work as quickly and as carefully as you can.

You can print **multiple-choice answer sheets** for these questions from our website — go to cgpbooks.co.uk/11plus/answer-sheets or scan the QR code on the right. If you'd prefer to answer the questions on the page, just follow the instructions in the question.

Answer Sheets

> Read this passage carefully and answer the questions that follow.

An extract from 'A Master of Djinn*'

Archibald James Portendorf disliked stairs. With their ludicrous lengths, ever leading up, as if in some jest. There were times, he thought, he could even hear them snickering. If these stairs had eyes to see, they would do more than snicker — watching as he huffed through curling auburn whiskers, his short legs wobbling under his rotundity. It was criminal in this modern age that stairs
5 should be allowed to yet exist — when lifts could carry passengers in comfort.

He stopped to rest against a giant replica of a copper teapot with a curving spout like a beak, setting down the burden he'd been carrying. It was shameful that someone of his years, having reached sixty and one in this year 1912, should suffer such indignities. He should be settling down for the night with a stiff drink, not trotting up a set of ruddy stairs!
10 "All for king, country, and company," he muttered.

Mopping sweat from his forehead, he wished he could reach the dampness lining his back and other unmentionable regions that his dark suit, by fortune, hid away. It was warm for November, and in this overheated land it seemed his body no longer knew how *not* to sweat. With a sigh, he turned weary eyes to an arched window. At this hour he could still make out the sloping outline
15 of the pyramids, the stone shining beneath a full moon that hung luminous in the black sky.

Egypt. The mysterious jewel of the Orient, land of pharaohs, fabled Mamlukes*, and countless marvels. For ten long years now, Archibald had spent three, four, even six months in the country at a time. And one thing was certain: he'd had his fill.

*Djinn — *a spirit in Arabic mythology*   **by P. Djèlí Clark**
*Mamlukes — *enslaved soldiers*

> Answer these questions about the text that you've just read.
> Circle the letter of the correct answer.

1. Which of these best describes Archibald?

   A Generous and cheerful
   B Anxious and thoughtful
   C Vengeful and unreasonable
   D Bitter and uncomfortable
   E Embarrassed and upset

2. "It was criminal in this modern age that stairs should be allowed to yet exist" (lines 4-5). What is meant by this?

   A Stairs need to be properly approved before they are built.
   B It is unjust that people still have to use stairs.
   C There are not many stairs in Egypt.
   D Stairs have recently been made illegal in Egypt.
   E Stairs used to be illegal in Egypt.

/ 2

Carry on to the next question → →

3. Which of the following statements is true?

   A Archibald is taking something up the stairs.
   B Archibald is going up the stairs to go to bed.
   C Archibald is trying to exercise by going up the stairs.
   D Archibald is going up the stairs to get a good view of the pyramids.
   E Archibald is going up the stairs to meet the king.

4. Why does Archibald think he should not "suffer such indignities" (line 8)?

   A He is too tired.
   B He is too unfit.
   C He is too thirsty.
   D He is too warm.
   E He is too old.

5. Which of the following is not mentioned in the text?

   A What colour Archibald's facial hair is.
   B What time of day it is.
   C What Archibald would rather be doing.
   D What reason Archibald has for being in Egypt.
   E What time of year it is.

6. The text describes Egypt as the "jewel of the Orient" (line 16). What does this mean?

   A Egypt is the most treasured country in that area.
   B Egypt has the biggest diamond mines of any country in that area.
   C Egypt contains the most gems of any country in that area.
   D Egypt is the biggest country in that area.
   E Egypt is the most technologically advanced country in that area.

7. For how long has Archibald been making visits to Egypt?

   A Half a century
   B A decade
   C Half a year
   D Three months
   E One month

8. "And one thing was certain: he'd had his fill" (line 18). What does this sentence mean?

   A Archibald wants to keep going to Egypt.
   B Archibald has eaten plenty of food in Egypt.
   C Archibald has spent lots of money in Egypt.
   D Archibald has had a lot of fun in Egypt.
   E Archibald is ready to stop going to Egypt.

/ 6

Answer these questions about the way words and phrases are used in the passage.

9. Which of these words is closest in meaning to "ludicrous" (line 1)?

   A Enormous
   B Hazardous
   C Continuous
   D Ridiculous
   E Mountainous

10. What does the word "replica" (line 6) mean?

   A Carving
   B Sculpture
   C Decoration
   D Painting
   E Copy

11. The word "fabled" (line 16) could most accurately be replaced by:

   A wise.
   B legendary.
   C traditional.
   D overrated.
   E hard-working.

12. "There were times, he thought, he could even hear them snickering" (line 2). What is this sentence an example of?

   A Personification
   B A proverb
   C A metaphor
   D Alliteration
   E A synonym

13. What technique is used in the phrase "with a curving spout like a beak" (line 6)?

   A Onomatopoeia
   B Irony
   C Metaphor
   D Simile
   E Personification

14. What type of words are these?

   snicker exist carry suffer

   A Adjectives
   B Adverbs
   C Verbs
   D Proper nouns
   E Pronouns

/ 6

Carry on to the next question → →

Assessment Test 5

Read this passage carefully and answer the questions that follow.

Recycling

Recycling is an excellent way to cut down on the colossal amounts of waste destined for landfill every year. Plenty of household materials can be processed into something new — I bet that in the past day alone, you've used multiple items that can be recycled. The growing recycling industry has many benefits — it offers employment, conserves crucial resources and cuts down on the pollution
5   caused by landfill sites. As well as this, turning existing products into new ones generally uses less energy and emits less carbon dioxide than making them from scratch.

Paper and metal are the two most recycled materials in the UK, in part because of the ease with which they can be recycled. Metals, for example, are sorted into different types, often using a magnet. The metal then passes through a shredder before being melted at very high temperatures
10   and formed into bars, ready to be reused where needed. Plastics, however, see a much lower percentage of recycling, and the picture for other materials is even worse.

So why don't some materials get recycled as much? If, like me, you've felt the shame of resorting to using regular waste bins when out and about, you'll know that it's not always convenient to carry packaging home with you — although we know this shouldn't stop us. Something else
15   that might contribute to the low levels of recycling is that people may not know what materials are actually recyclable. Things like timber and ceramics, although not accepted in household recycling bins, can often be taken to local recycling centres which are suited to dealing with them.

Of course, the responsibility for recycling shouldn't lie solely with the individual. Big companies should always strive to enhance their sustainability. As well as finding ways to recycle more, this
20   could also involve reducing the volume of waste that is produced in the first place.

Answer these questions about the text that you've just read.
Circle the letter of the correct answer.

15. Which of these is not given as an advantage of recycling?

   A   It doesn't cost a lot of money.
   B   It reduces the need to extract new materials.
   C   It reduces pollution.
   D   It creates job opportunities.
   E   It uses less energy than making new products.

16. According to the text, what might stop people from recycling?

   A   They forget to do it.
   B   They don't have the time.
   C   They are not aware that a material can be recycled.
   D   They don't think it is good to recycle.
   E   Recycling is not collected from people's homes.

/ 2

17. According to the text, why is paper widely recycled?

   A Because it is fairly easy to recycle.
   B Because it has been recycled for a long time.
   C Because the government is responsible for recycling it.
   D Because people get paid for recycling it.
   E Because paper can be separated easily.

18. According to the text, when metal is recycled it is:

   A separated and cleaned.
   B weighed and magnetised.
   C broken apart and dried.
   D heated and reshaped.
   E washed and crushed.

19. How do you think the author feels about their recycling habits?

   A Upset
   B Pleased
   C Smug
   D Relieved
   E Guilty

20. According to the text, wood:

   A can be recycled in household bins.
   B should be burned at home.
   C cannot be recycled.
   D should be taken to specialist recycling centres.
   E should be composted in the garden.

21. According to the text, which of these statements is true?

   A More paper is recycled than plastic in the UK.
   B Companies are legally required to invest in sustainability.
   C Recycling does not release any carbon dioxide.
   D Ceramics cannot be recycled in the UK.
   E Metals are the least recycled material in the UK.

22. The author says that "the responsibility for recycling shouldn't lie solely with the individual" (line 18). What does this mean?

   A Individuals need to pressure companies to recycle.
   B Both individuals and organisations should recycle.
   C Organisations generate more recycling than individuals.
   D Individual households are generally good at recycling.
   E Organisations need to set an example to individuals.

/ 6

52

Answer these questions about the way words and phrases are used in the passage.

23. Which of these words is closest in meaning to "colossal" (line 1)?

   A Worrying
   B Enormous
   C Disappointing
   D Unbelievable
   E Frustrating

24. What does the word "crucial" (line 4) mean?

   A Basic
   B Urgent
   C Meaningful
   D Essential
   E Useful

25. The phrase "contribute to" (line 15) could most accurately be replaced by:

   A play a part in.
   B help increase.
   C prevent shrinking.
   D be a result of.
   E better regulate.

26. Which of these words is closest in meaning to "enhance" (line 19)?

   A Change
   B Improve
   C Sharpen
   D Refine
   E Promote

27. "So why don't some materials get recycled as much?" (line 12) is an example of what technique?

   A A cliché
   B Personification
   C A proverb
   D Onomatopoeia
   E A rhetorical question

28. What type of word is "recyclable" (line 16)?

   A Adverb
   B Verb
   C Adjective
   D Common noun
   E Collective noun

/ 6

Total / 28

End of Test

Assessment Test 5

Assessment Test 6

Allow 28 minutes to do this test and work as quickly and as carefully as you can.

You can print **multiple-choice answer sheets** for these questions from our website — go to cgpbooks.co.uk/11plus/answer-sheets or scan the QR code on the right. If you'd prefer to answer the questions on the page, just follow the instructions in the question.

Answer
Sheets

Read this passage carefully and answer the questions that follow.

The Volunteer

As their car crunched along the sweeping driveway, Kie let out a deep sigh and picked at a hole in the knee of his jeans. Only when his dad had ushered him out of the vehicle, given him a final terse warning to behave himself, and driven away, did he study the building before him. Built on a grand scale from weathered, golden stone that seemed to radiate soft light, and veiled with some
5 sort of flowering vine, it was an elegant structure. Eyes widening, Kie swallowed heavily, then he gave a short bark of laughter and kicked at the gravel, leaving a long scuff in its pristine surface.

Slouching unhurriedly towards the open front door, he noticed an elderly man watching him from the shadow of the porch. Kie averted his gaze as he passed the man. He scorned old people with their irritating questions and tedious stories — doubtless that was why Dad had insisted that
10 he volunteer here. No chance of him helping to plant trees, rewild wasteland or some other activity that he might have enjoyed even slightly. No. He was stuck here with dozens of people who were probably too ancient to do anything but drink tea, play bingo and reminisce about rationing.

As he loitered in the care home's reception, Kie heard a commotion coming from a side room. Curious despite himself, he glanced left and right, then eased open the heavy door. Peering inside,
15 he suppressed an exclamation. Before him, in a loose knot, stood nine or ten senior citizens, some clutching controllers and all staring at a huge, state-of-the-art plasma screen on which sleek cars hurtled around a racetrack. A vehement debate seemed to be underway about whether to use turbo mode or jet boosters. Kie marched into the room. *I can help with this*, he thought.

Answer these questions about the text that you've just read.
Circle the letter of the correct answer.

1. Which of the following best describes the building?

   A Large, with a long pebbled drive
   B Large, with a smart tarmac drive
   C Small, with a long pebbled drive
   D Small, with a smart tarmac drive
   E Moderately sized, with no drive

2. Which of the following best describes Kie's feelings in lines 5-6?

   A He feels bored, then rebellious.
   B He feels annoyed, then eager to go inside.
   C He feels overwhelmed, then terrified.
   D He feels nervous, then unconcerned.
   E He feels hopeful, then apprehensive.

/ 2

Carry on to the next question →→

54

3. According to the text, why doesn't Kie respect old people?

   A He finds their stories about war disturbing.
   B He thinks they are annoying and boring.
   C He believes they drink too much tea.
   D He thinks they are suspicious of young people.
   E He dislikes the way they gather in large groups.

4. Which of the following statements is true?

   A Kie has volunteered at this care home before.
   B Kie's dad is not strict with Kie.
   C Kie is smartly dressed.
   D Kie's dad chose where Kie would volunteer.
   E Kie arrives at the care home on foot.

5. Which of these best describes how Kie feels about volunteering to help with environmental conservation?

   A He would love to do it because he is passionate about the environment.
   B He thinks he would prefer it to volunteering in the care home.
   C He dislikes being outside, so would rather not do it.
   D He believes it would be even more boring than the care home.
   E He views it as a worthwhile but boring thing to do.

6. Why do you think Kie "eased open the heavy door" (line 14)?

   A He isn't strong enough to open it quickly.
   B He thinks whatever is in the room might be dangerous.
   C The door is very stiff and hard to open.
   D He thinks there might be someone behind it.
   E He doesn't want anyone to notice him.

7. Kie "suppressed an exclamation" (line 15).
   What does this suggest?

   A He has hurt himself opening the door.
   B He is surprised by what he sees.
   C He is shocked that the room is full of people.
   D He is annoyed at having to help people.
   E He has seen someone he knows.

8. Which of the following options best describes what the senior citizens are doing in lines 15-18?

   A They are discussing how to work the controllers.
   B They are watching a television programme.
   C They are arguing about a computer game.
   D They are playing a board game.
   E They are debating the best make of television.

/ 6

Answer these questions about the way words and phrases are used in the passage.

9. Which of these words is closest in meaning to "terse" (line 2)?

   A Rude
   B Hurried
   C Angry
   D Abrupt
   E Desperate

10. Which of these words is closest in meaning to "pristine" (line 6)?

   A Immaculate
   B Polished
   C Sparkling
   D Uncluttered
   E Respectable

11. The word "loitered" (line 13) could most accurately be replaced by:

   A sulked
   B listened
   C daydreamed
   D pondered
   E idled

12. The car "crunched along the sweeping driveway" (line 1).
    What technique is used here?

   A Alliteration
   B Onomatopoeia
   C Abbreviation
   D Personification
   E Irony

13. What type of words are these?

   deep   weathered   ancient   sleek

   A Adverbs
   B Verbs
   C Adjectives
   D Prepositions
   E Conjunctions

14. What type of word is "rewild" (line 10)?

   A Common noun
   B Adjective
   C Adverb
   D Abstract noun
   E Verb

/ 6

Carry on to the next question → →

Read this poem carefully and answer the questions that follow.

Street Cries

When dawn's first cymbals beat upon the sky,
Rousing the world to labour's various cry,
To tend the flock, to bind the mellowing grain,
From ardent toil to forge a little gain,
5 And fasting men go forth on hurrying feet,
BUY BREAD, BUY BREAD, rings down the
        eager street.

When the earth falters and the waters swoon
With the implacable* radiance of noon,
And in dim shelters koils* hush their notes,
10 And the faint, thirsting blood in languid* throats
Craves liquid succour* from the cruel heat,
BUY FRUIT, BUY FRUIT, steals down the
        panting street.

When twilight twinkling o'er the gay bazaars,
Unfurls a sudden canopy of stars,
15 When lutes* are strung and fragrant torches lit
On white roof-terraces where lovers sit
Drinking together of life's poignant sweet,
BUY FLOWERS, BUY FLOWERS, floats down
        the singing street.

by Sarojini Naidu

*ardent — *dedicated*
*implacable — *relentless*
*koils — *birds in the cuckoo family*
*languid — *having little energy*
*succour — *relief*
*lutes — *stringed instruments*

Answer these questions about the text that you've just read.
Circle the letter of the correct answer.

15. How much time passes during the poem?

 A An hour
 B A day
 C A week
 D A year
 E A lifetime

16. According to the poem, how are people woken up?

 A By people shouting in the street
 B By music playing outside
 C By alarm bells ringing
 D By the sounds of early morning
 E By loud cracks of thunder

/ 2

17. According to line 4 of the poem, why do people work?

    A So they can buy food
    B To improve their lives
    C Because they love their jobs
    D To create products
    E For the sense of achievement

18. "And fasting men go forth on hurrying feet" (line 5).
    What does this suggest about the men?

    A They are excited to get to work.
    B They want to get home quickly.
    C They are rushing to their jobs as street sellers.
    D They are training for a race.
    E They haven't eaten for some time.

19. Which of the following best describes conditions in the second verse?

    A Hot and dry
    B Bright and cool
    C Dark and shady
    D Mild and sunny
    E Warm and humid

20. Which of the following statements about the third verse (lines 13-18) is false?

    A There is music.
    B People sit in pairs.
    C There is soft light.
    D People drink wine.
    E The sky is clear.

21. The first verse of the poem suggests the presence of people doing different jobs.
    Which of the following workers are present in the first verse?

    A Farmer, blacksmith, artist
    B Teacher, chef, shepherd
    C Artist, baker, teacher
    D Farmer, shepherd, baker
    E Athlete, blacksmith, chef

22. Why do the cries of the street sellers change in each verse?

    A It reveals what goods the sellers have left.
    B It emphasises the long hours the sellers work.
    C It reflects the way people's desires change.
    D It hints that the sellers are becoming desperate.
    E It suggests that the sellers don't stay in one place.

/ 6

Answer these questions about the way words and phrases are used in the passage.

23. Which of these words is closest in meaning to "swoon" (line 7)?

    A Dive
    B Rest
    C Faint
    D Flow
    E Boil

24. The word "Craves" (line 11) could most accurately be replaced by:

    A desires.
    B envisions.
    C demands.
    D gains.
    E hunts.

25. "BUY FRUIT, BUY FRUIT, steals down the panting street" (line 12).
    This is an example of:

    A a simile.
    B irony.
    C an oxymoron.
    D personification.
    E an analogy.

26. "a sudden canopy of stars" (line 14).
    What technique is being used here?

    A Onomatopoeia
    B A metaphor
    C A cliché
    D A simile
    E Abbreviation

27. What type of words are "cry" (line 2) and "toil" (line 4)?

    A Adverbs
    B Verbs
    C Adjectives
    D Nouns
    E Pronouns

28. "On white roof-terraces where lovers sit" (line 16).
    Which word in this sentence is an adjective?

    A white
    B roof
    C where
    D lovers
    E sit

/ 6

Total   / 28

End of Test

Assessment Test 7

Allow 28 minutes to do this test and work as quickly and as carefully as you can.

You can print **multiple-choice answer sheets** for these questions from our website — go to cgpbooks.co.uk/11plus/answer-sheets or scan the QR code on the right. If you'd prefer to answer the questions on the page, just follow the instructions in the question.

Read this poem carefully and answer the questions that follow.

Swimming Lessons

The first time father sent him in,
Waves struck him like a drum.
Pink and frozen flesh went numb,
As salt's sting kissed keen eye and skin.

5 Billowing lungs seared and strained,
While weeds reached out for flailing limbs,
As chattering, clattering teeth all grinned,
And winced from icy pain.

Above, gulls teased with mewling caws
10 As the son found the waves' rhythm at last.
He bobbed in time and, steady but not fast,
He toiled shoreward, to fatherly applause.

The last time father sees him dive in,
He arcs and soars straight down.
15 Wiser, full-grown and fearless now,
Chlorine's sting prompts just a grin.

Firm, confident kicks propel,
While lanes restrict the routes ahead,
And silent ripples slowly spread,
20 The token of an art learnt well.

Now, pool pumps' constant, whirring thrum
Echoes within the man, who thrusts,
Strokes, glides and powers on — who trusts
Himself and all he has become.

Answer these questions about the text that you've just read.
Circle the letter of the correct answer.

1. Which of the following statements about the father is false?

   A He encouraged his son to swim in the sea.
   B He observed his son from a distance.
   C He praised his son when he succeeded.
   D He showed his son proper swimming technique.
   E He watched his son at swimming events.

2. Which of these is not mentioned in the poem?

   A Ocean waves
   B Bird calls
   C Armbands
   D Seaweed
   E Swimming pools

/ 2

Carry on to the next question → →

3. What do lines 5-8 focus on?

   A How the son floated in the water.
   B What makes deep water so dangerous.
   C Why you shouldn't swim at high tide.
   D The physical sensation of being in the sea.
   E What inspired the son to swim.

4. The poet describes an "icy pain" (line 8).
   What do you think this is caused by?

   A The seaweed wrapping around the son's legs.
   B The son's teeth bashing together as he shivered.
   C The chill of the seawater on the son's skin.
   D The piercing shriek of the gulls flying overhead.
   E The discomfort of swallowing cold seawater.

5. Which detail suggests that the son could become a skilled swimmer?

   A He instinctively started moving in time with the waves.
   B His father clapped as he slowly swam back to the beach.
   C He made careful observations while struggling to swim.
   D He summoned an extra burst of energy when he needed it.
   E He smiled when the water first touched his skin.

6. How is the son's attitude to swimming different in the second half of the poem?

   A He only swims in heated pools.
   B He starts showing off when people watch him swim.
   C He prefers to swim without making a sound.
   D He sees swimming as the only important thing in life.
   E He feels comfortable in the water.

7. Which of the following statements about the son in the second half of the poem is true?

   A He is an adult.
   B He is an Olympic athlete.
   C He is a competitive diver.
   D He is a father.
   E He is on a swimming team.

8. "Now, pool pumps' constant, whirring thrum / Echoes within the man" (lines 21-22).
   What does this tell us about the son?

   A He is sensitive to loud noises.
   B He has a well-maintained swimming pool.
   C He is at one with his surroundings.
   D He has a keen sense of hearing.
   E He ignores distractions while swimming.

/ 6

Answer these questions about the way words and phrases are used in the passage.

9. Which of these words is closest in meaning to "prompts" (line 16)?

   A Infers
   B Infects
   C Infuses
   D Induces
   E Inhibits

10. The word "arcs" (line 14) could most accurately be replaced by:

   A tumbles.
   B curves.
   C twists.
   D coils.
   E leaps.

11. Which of these words is closest in meaning to "token" (line 20)?

   A Appearance
   B Indicator
   C Guarantee
   D Reward
   E Omen

12. "While lanes restrict the routes ahead" (line 18).
    What type of word is "While"?

   A Adverb
   B Adjective
   C Preposition
   D Conjunction
   E Verb

13. "As salt's sting kissed keen eye and skin" (line 4). This is an example of:

   A a cliché.
   B a proverb.
   C an idiom.
   D a simile.
   E personification.

14. "Above, gulls teased with mewling caws" (line 9). What technique is used here?

   A Onomatopoeia
   B Simile
   C Metaphor
   D Irony
   E Alliteration

/ 6

Carry on to the next question → →

Assessment Test 7

The Cat

Bogdan snapped upright with a whimper. He usually relished the night and the freedom of movement it brought, but tonight rivers of sweat coursed down his quivering back, seeping into his once-crisp shirt. The now-familiar nightmare had enveloped him like a haunting, wintry cloud the second he'd closed his eyes. *Cursed.* He knew he must be — he'd not slept for two days now, ever
5 since the heist, and the prospect of trying again tonight turned his blood to ice even as perspiration beaded his flushed skin.

Rising, Bogdan stole across the dusty mosaic floor of the abandoned theatre he'd called his home for the past week. It wasn't really a home, of course. Nor was it, strictly speaking, 'his'. It was empty, far from other dwellings and comfortably off-grid. In short, it was everything Bogdan looked for in a
10 base of operations. He drew the sickly white plastic of the cracked, wall-mounted telephone towards him and cradled the receiver to his ear. Fingers poised to dial, he paused.

I should report this, he thought. *But... they'll think I'm being dramatic, or that I'm some superstitious fool, or worse: they'll realise I'm afraid.* Bogdan hurriedly hung the phone back up. That wouldn't do at all. He couldn't risk his reputation being tainted by such rumours — Bogdan Lisák, the Feline Felon,
15 master thief — afraid? No. He'd have to handle this himself.

Stalking over to the far corner of the once-grand foyer, he brushed his hair from his sea-green, almond-shaped eyes and stared down at the shunned source of his woe. The sleek velvet pouch seemed to glow in the starlight that crept in through the dilapidated ceiling, unsettling Bogdan. He upended the bag onto a desk nearby, taking care to avoid touching the stone that tumbled out. The
20 surrounding shadows seemed to flex as the amethyst came to rest. Greedily, the gem inhaled even more of the dim light, until all Bogdan saw, or rather, *felt*, was its ominous aura, beckoning him closer. It felt seductive. It felt powerful. It felt dark.

Bogdan swallowed heavily. Two realisations sprang into his mind at once. First: his employers must have known that this target came with additional, supernatural peril. Why else would they have
25 offered a king's ransom for a single item? Second: he should not have taken the job.

---

15. Why does Bogdan think that he is "*Cursed*" (line 4)?

   A He sees ghosts every time he closes his eyes.
   B He hasn't been able to rest for several days.
   C He feels both hot and cold at the same time.
   D He senses a freezing-cold cloud all around him.
   E He has several terrifying nightmares each night.

16. Why did Bogdan set up his base in the abandoned theatre?

   A It is a beautiful and historic old building.
   B It contains dark corners and secret entryways.
   C It allows him to sleep underneath the stars.
   D It is well-furnished and secluded.
   E It is uninhabited and remote.

/ 2

17. Which of the following adjectives best describes Bogdan's movements in the story?

   A Relaxed
   B Sprightly
   C Coordinated
   D Stealthy
   E Energetic

18. Which of the following is not mentioned in the story?

   A A theft
   B A dream
   C A friend
   D A jewel
   E A mosaic

19. Which of the following does Bogdan show in lines 23-25?

   A Humility
   B Acceptance
   C Anger
   D Regret
   E Foresight

20. The title of the story refers to Bogdan.
    Which of the following cat-like traits does Bogdan not display?

   A Being active at night.
   B Having green eyes.
   C Behaving playfully.
   D Being wary of people.
   E Seeming to sense danger.

21. Why do you think Bogdan stores the stolen pouch in "the far corner" (line 16)?

   A He doesn't want to be found with stolen goods near his person.
   B He knows that its contents are dangerous and doesn't want it near him.
   C He thinks the pouch looks more impressive by starlight.
   D He keeps the pouch near the desk so that he can inspect its contents more easily.
   E He wants the dark shadows of the corner to conceal the pouch.

22. What kind of mood does the author create in lines 20-22?

   A Threatening
   B Anguished
   C Sorrowful
   D Agitated
   E Anxious

/ 6

Carry on to the next question → →

64

Answer these questions about the way words and phrases are used in the passage.

23. What type of word is "prospect" (line 5)?

   A Verb
   B Adverb
   C Preposition
   D Adjective
   E Noun

24. Which of these words is closest in meaning to "poised" (line 11)?

   A Assured
   B Eager
   C Ready
   D Prone
   E Willing

25. "rivers of sweat coursed down his quivering back" (line 2). What technique is used here?

   A Simile
   B Analogy
   C Onomatopoeia
   D Metaphor
   E Personification

26. Which of these words could most accurately replace "dilapidated" (line 18)?

   A Crumbling
   B Exposed
   C Collapsed
   D Outdated
   E Defective

27. "Greedily, the gem inhaled even more of the dim light" (lines 20-21). This is an example of:

   A onomatopoeia.
   B alliteration.
   C a simile.
   D irony.
   E personification.

28. What technique is used in the phrase "a king's ransom" (line 25)?

   A Irony
   B Idiom
   C Simile
   D Proverb
   E Analogy

/ 6

Total   / 28

End of Test

Glossary

abbreviation	A shortened version of a word, e.g. "bike" instead of "bicycle".
abstract noun	A word that names something you can't see, hear, touch, smell or taste, e.g. "happiness".
adjective	A word that describes a noun, e.g. "beautiful morning", "frosty lawn".
adverb	A word that describes a verb or an adjective, e.g. "He ran quickly."
alliteration	The repetition of a sound at the beginning of words within a phrase, e.g. "Lovely Lois likes lipstick."
analogy	A comparison to show how one thing is similar to another, which makes it easier to understand or remember. E.g. "watching cricket is about as exciting as watching paint dry."
antonym	A word that has the opposite meaning to another, e.g. "good" and "bad".
cliché	A phrase that has been overused and has lost some of its impact, e.g. "Avoid it like the plague."
collective noun	A word that names a group of things, e.g. "bunch", "herd", "batch".
common noun	A word that names things in general, e.g. "woman", "table", "monkey".
concrete noun	A word that names something you can see, hear, touch, smell or taste, e.g. "bread".
conjunction	A word that joins two clauses, e.g. "and", "but".
fiction	Text that has been made up by the author, about imaginary people and events.
idiom	A phrase which doesn't literally mean what it says, e.g. "raining cats and dogs".
imagery	Language that creates a vivid picture in the reader's mind.
irony	When a writer says the opposite of what they mean, or when the opposite happens to what the reader expects.
metaphor	A way of describing something by saying that it is something else, e.g. "John's legs were lead weights."
non-fiction	Text that is about facts and real people and events.
noun	A word that names something, e.g. "Paul", "scissors", "flock", "loyalty".
onomatopoeia	When words sound like the noise they describe, e.g. "pop", "bang", "squelch".
personification	A way of describing something by giving it human feelings and characteristics, e.g. "The cruel wind plucked remorselessly at my threadbare clothes."
preposition	A word that tells you how things are related, e.g. "in", "above", "before", "of".
pronoun	Words that can be used instead of nouns, e.g. "I", "you", "he", "it".
proper noun	A word that names a particular person, place or thing, e.g. "Heather", "Rome", "Monday".
proverb	A short well-known saying that may give advice, e.g. "There's no point crying over spilt milk."
rhetorical question	A question that doesn't need an answer, e.g. "When will they learn?"
simile	A way of describing something by comparing it to something else, e.g. "The stars were like a thousand diamonds, glittering in the sky."
synonym	A word with a similar meaning to another word, e.g. "big" and "huge".
verb	An action or being word, e.g. "I run", "he went", "you are".

Answers

Section One — Information and Ideas

Page 2 — Finding Facts

1) **False** — In the passage it says that a kingfisher is "marginally bigger than a robin" (lines 3-4). This means that kingfishers are not the same size as robins.

2) **True** — The passage says that kingfishers can be seen "alongside a river" (line 5).

3) **False** — The passage mentions that kingfishers "may resort to feeding on beetles and other insects" (lines 11-12). This means they sometimes eat food other than fish.

4) **False** — The passage says that "some kingfishers survive by migrating" (line 12), but that others change their food sources instead. This means that not all kingfishers migrate.

5) **e.g.** "you might occasionally glimpse one" (line 4). The word "occasionally" suggests it is not common to see a kingfisher.

6) **e.g.** "an impressive speed of up to 40 km per hour" (lines 7-8). This shows that they move very quickly when diving.

7) **e.g.** "freshwater freezes and kingfishers struggle to find food" (lines 10-11). This means that when ice forms in winter, it's harder for kingfishers to catch fish to eat.

Page 3 — Finding Facts

1) **C** — The passage says that Hall was born "in 1901" (line 1). This is in the 20th century.

2) **C** — The passage mentions that scat singing is a "style of jazz singing" (line 2) and that "the voice mimics an instrument" (line 3) when scatting. The text doesn't mention when scatting was first introduced.

3) **B** — The passage mentions that Hall had "success on both sides of the Atlantic" (line 7), which means she did well in both the USA and the UK.

4) **C** — The passage explains that Hall "performed" in order to "boost Londoners' morale" (lines 10-11), which means that she sang to make people feel better.

5) **A** — The passage says that Hall's popularity "never entirely died out" (line 12) and lists some of the work she did later in her career. This shows that she continued to be successful.

Page 4 — Finding Facts

1) **Tia's** — The text says "Tia had initially proposed this trip" (line 2). This means that going camping was Tia's idea.

2) **Her telescope** — The text says that Tia found the tent while she was "trying to unearth her prized telescope" (line 3).

3) **A weekend** — The text says that the tent will be their "home for the weekend" (line 6).

4) **30 minutes** — The text says that pitching the tent took "half an hour" (line 9), which is 30 minutes.

5) **e.g.** "their shabby tent" (lines 2). "shabby" means 'in poor condition'.

6) **e.g.** "the tattered instructions that were just about legible" (line 8). "legible" means 'clear enough to read', so the instructions were only just clear enough to read.

7) **e.g.** "countless streaks of light" (line 13). The "streaks of light" in the sky are meteors, and the fact that they are "countless" means there are a lot of them.

Page 5 — Finding Facts

1) **C** — The poem says "Our journey dawns as the sun descends" (line 1) and goes on to mention the "dying light" (line 11). This shows that it is evening because the sun is setting.

2) **A** — The poem describes "scarlet hues" (line 2), "emerald meadows" (line 3) and "Milk-white pyramids" (line 10), but it does not mention any shade of blue.

3) **C** — The poem says that the deer are "Far too swift" (line 8). This suggests that the deer move rapidly out of view.

4) **B** — The phrase "Snow-capped" (line 9) means that only the tops of the mountains have snow on them because 'cap' refers to the top of something.

5) **C** — The narrator mentions feeling "forlorn" (line 13), which means 'sad', and that they are returning to a "city" (line 16). They also describe the "meadows" (line 3) and "mountains" (line 9) they pass, but they do not mention where in the train they are sitting.

Answers

Page 6 — Finding Hidden Facts

1) **Happy** — The fact that Mia "basked" (line 1) in the sun and the exclamation mark after "A whole day to herself" (lines 2-3) suggest she is enjoying her time alone.

2) **Unconcerned** — Mia "instinctively" avoids the creaky floorboard and "Absentmindedly" (line 9) opens the tricky front door, which suggests that she does not really notice these flaws.

3) **Irritated** — Mia gives "a deep sigh" and gets up "reluctantly" (line 8), which suggests she is annoyed by the interruption.

4) **Confused** — The passage says "Mia looked up and down the road" (line 13) and describes the delivery person as "mysterious" (line 15). This suggests she is confused because she doesn't know who has brought her flowers or why.

5) **annoyed** — e.g. Mia is tired of listening to Reece "complaining" (line 4).

6) **a town** — e.g. Mia can hear "the cries of market vendors" (line 14), which are more likely to be found in a town.

Page 7 — Finding Hidden Facts

1) **C** — The flags are "nearly blending in with the clear summer sky" (line 4), and in good weather the colour of the sky is blue.

2) **C** — Jamal describes the marathon as an "ordeal" (line 5), but the passage doesn't mention the other runners' supporters or who received their water first.

3) **B** — The passage says that when Jamal received his water, he "emptied it over his head" (line 8), which suggests that he feels very hot.

4) **A** — The woman is "smiling" (line 5) at Jamal, and reminds him of his mum, who is encouraging and "supportive" (line 10).

5) **B** — Jamal says "I'll see you on the other side" (line 13), which shows that he believes he can finish the marathon.

Page 8 — Finding Hidden Facts

1) **e.g.** "a landmark for those entering the area by car" (line 4). Cars will be entering the area by road, so the Angel must be visible from nearby roads.

2) **e.g.** "this steel weathers over time, producing a rusty hue" (line 7). Steel is usually a grey colour, which suggests that the "special type of steel" (line 7) was specifically chosen because it would eventually turn the statue a dark shade of orange.

3) **distinctive** — e.g. The statue is described as "recognisable" (line 13), which suggests that it stands out.

4) **positive** — e.g. The writer describes the statue as "spectacular" (line 15), which suggests they admire it.

Page 9 — Finding Hidden Facts

1) **C** — The poem mentions the "age-old legend" (line 5) of the ghost ship, which means the ship must have been wrecked a long time ago.

2) **A** — The poem suggests that making any noise will mean "we too would run aground" (line 8), which suggests the sailors are afraid of a curse on the ghost ship.

3) **C** — The poem says the crew "did not stir" (line 19) as the ghost ship was wrecked, so they did not try to steer it out to sea.

4) **A** — The poem mentions the sailors' "grief" (line 11) and "unshed tears" (line 21), which suggests they feel sorry for the lost crew.

Page 10 — Interpreting Quotes

1) **e.g.** "Elias tore along the endless, winding corridors" (line 1). The word "tore" means 'moved very quickly'.

2) **e.g.** "he pirouetted" (line 3). The verb "pirouetted" likens Elias to a dancer, showing that he is agile.

3) **e.g.** "a flicker of hope danced in Elias's heart" (line 7). This image shows Elias's belief that he can make it in time.

4) **e.g.** The gaps Elias squeezed through were tiny — A "half-starved rat" is very thin, so gaps it thinks are "ambitious" must be very small.

Answers

5) **e.g.** Elias feels so upset that he struggles to stand — In this context, "buckled" means 'folded', so the quote suggests that he is so distressed he starts to sag towards the floor.

6) **e.g.** The door makes a groaning sound — Asthma is a condition that affects breathing, so "an asthmatic wheeze" is a noise like someone struggling to draw breath.

Page 11 — Interpreting Quotes

1) **B** — "adored" means 'loved', so this phrase means it's liked very much by a lot of people.

2) **C** — "fortuitous" means 'lucky', and the text suggests that carbonara was invented because the right circumstances arose.

3) **B** — In this sentence, the phrase "inclined to stress" means 'likely to draw attention to', so the supporters of this theory are emphasising something that supports their argument.

4) **A** — "abundance" means 'a large quantity of something', so it is referring to the amount of pepper in carbonara.

5) **A** — The phrase "the whole is greater than the sum of its parts" means that when you add all the elements of something together, they combine to create something much better. So carbonara is better than its individual ingredients.

Page 12 — Word Meanings

1) **Overpowering** — "Irresistible" means 'overpowering'. Both words mean 'impossible to refuse'.

2) **Basic** — "Primitive" means 'basic'. Both words mean 'simple and undeveloped'.

3) **Pointless** — "Futile" means 'pointless'. Both words mean 'without purpose'.

4) **Stimulating** — "Inspiring" means 'stimulating'. Both words mean 'causing creative feelings'.

5) **Beautiful** — "Exquisite" means 'beautiful'. Both words mean 'lovely to look at'.

6) **Clumsy** — 'Ungainly' means "clumsy" (line 6). Both words mean 'awkward'.

7) **Lethal** — 'Deadly' means "lethal" (line 11). Both words mean 'causing death'.

8) **Swirling** — 'Billowing' means "swirling" (line 2). Both words describe a flowing, twisting movement.

9) **Uninhabited** — 'Deserted' means "uninhabited" (line 19). Both words mean 'not occupied by people'.

10) **Fate** — 'Destiny' means "fate" (line 18). Both words mean 'unavoidable future events'.

Page 13 — Word Meanings

1) **C** — 'excitement' is closest in meaning to "exhilaration".

2) **B** — "clad" means the same as 'dressed'.

3) **D** — 'Secretively' is closest in meaning to "stealthily".

4) **B** — "tarnished" means the same as 'discoloured' here. Both words can mean 'dull'.

5) **D** — "warily" could most accurately be replaced by 'cautiously'.

6) **A** — 'enjoying' could most accurately replace "relishing".

Page 14 — Word Types

1) **verb** — "achieve" is a verb because it is an action word in the sentence.

2) **noun** — "darkness" is a noun because it is the name for 'the absence of light'.

3) **adverb** — "generally" is an adverb because it describes the verb "have".

4) **adjective** — "long" is an adjective because it describes the noun "time".

5) **successfully** — "successfully" is an adverb because it describes the verb "detect".

6) **objects** — "objects" is a concrete noun because it is the name for physical things than can be perceived by the five senses.

7) **Earth** — "Earth" is a proper noun because it is the name of a planet.

8) **to** — "to" is a preposition here because it shows how the noun "numbers" relates to the verb "fall".

Answers

Page 15 — Word Types

1) **B** — "over" is a preposition because it tells you where the narrator glanced.

2) **B** — "stifle" is a verb because it is an action word.

3) **D** — These words are abstract nouns because they are names for things that can't be experienced with your five senses.

4) **C** — "aware" is an adjective because it describes the pronoun "I".

5) **D** — "only" is an adverb because it describes the adjective "set".

Section Two — Writers' Techniques

Page 16 — Abbreviations

1) **approximately** — "approx" is an abbreviation for 'approximately'.

2) **kilometres** — "km" is an abbreviation for 'kilometres'.

3) **Mount** — "Mt" is an abbreviation for 'Mount'.

4) **temperature** — "temp" is an abbreviation for 'temperature'.

5) **Captain** — "Capt" is an abbreviation for 'Captain'.

6) **miles** — "mi" is an abbreviation for 'miles'.

7) **government** — "govt" is an abbreviation for 'government'.

8) **year** — "yr" is an abbreviation for 'year'.

Page 17 — Alliteration and Onomatopoeia

1) **B** — The phrase contains alliteration as the words "whisper" and "water" both begin with the 'w' sound.

2) **A** — "rumbling" sounds like the noise of a storm.

3) **D** — The phrase contains alliteration as the words "radiant" and "rose" both begin with the same 'r' sound.

4) **B** — "sputter" sounds like the noise of a series of soft explosions.

5) **D** — The phrase contains alliteration as the words "gentle" and "joy" both begin with the same 'j' sound.

6) **B** — "gulping" sounds like the noise something makes when it drinks quickly.

Page 18 — Imagery

1) **Simile** — This is a simile because humans are being compared to the wind.

2) **Metaphor** — This is a metaphor because the Emperor's rumbling stomach is described as an earthquake.

3) **Simile** — This is a simile because the animals are compared to arrows.

4) **Personification** — This is personification because the forest canopy is "generous" like a person.

5) **Simile** — This is a simile because the rabbit's realisation is compared to the sun.

6) **Metaphor** — This is a metaphor because the rabbit's nerves and heart are described as metals.

7) **Personification** — This is personification because the flames "licked hungrily", as if they were human.

8) **Simile** — This is a simile because the rabbit's spirit is compared to heaven.

Answers

Page 19 — Imagery

1) **C** — This is personification because the steel bars on the roller coaster carriage are described as human "arms" that "embrace" the people on the ride.

2) **B** — This is a metaphor because the hearts are described as stallions.

3) **B** — This is a simile because the colour of their knuckles is compared to snow.

4) **C** — This is personification because the "Goosebumps sprint", and sprinting is a human action.

5) **C** — This is a metaphor because the riders' excitement is described as a river that overflows.

Page 20 — Spotting and Understanding Devices

1) **Alliteration** — The 'b' sound is repeated at the beginning of "bedecked" and "baubles".

2) **Rhetorical question** — This is a rhetorical question because it is a question that you're not expected to answer.

3) **Idiom** — This is an idiom that means 'from nowhere'. The text uses this idiom to explain that people have been bringing greenery indoors during winter for a very long time.

4) **Simile** — This is a simile because the regrowth of plant life is compared to the arrival of hope.

5) **merrily dancing light** — This is personification because the "light" is described as "dancing" (line 7), which is a human activity.

6) **m** — In the phrase "70 m" (line 13), "m" is an abbreviation of 'metres'.

7) **installed** — "installed" (line 6) and 'placed' both mean 'put into position'.

8) **artificial** — "artificial" (line 12) and 'man-made' both mean 'synthetic'.

9) **delight** — 'displeasure' means 'disapproval', whereas "delight" (line 2) means 'pleasure'.

10) **increased** — 'reduced' means 'shrank', whereas "increased" (line 12) means 'grew'.

Page 21 — Spotting and Understanding Devices

1) **B** — This simile suggests that the tourists are being channelled in the same direction.

2) **D** — This metaphor suggests that the noises of the city create an energetic and cheerful piece of music.

3) **C** — Giving these smells makes it easier for the reader to imagine what the city smells like.

4) **B** — This simile suggests that the speaker feels like a crucial part of the city.

5) **A** — Naming several famous cities suggests that many other places may seem more interesting than the speaker's home.

Page 22 — Spotting and Understanding Devices

1) **isolated** — Ivy feels like an "uninhabitable island" (line 5), suggesting that she feels very alone.

2) **driftwood** — The boys were "bobbing" and "spinning" as they "eddied" (line 6) past Ivy, which is how driftwood travels on water currents.

3) **natural** — Ivy compares belonging to a group to "planets in a solar system" and "bees in a hive" (line 8), which are natural things.

4) **C** — Tortoises pull their heads back into their shells when they feel threatened, so this description suggests that Ivy feels exposed.

5) **B** — Trying to be sociable seems to take a lot of effort, which suggests the boy doesn't do it often.

6) **B** — The onomatopoeic "shrieks and whoops" are noises of excitement, which suggests that the playground has a happy, lively atmosphere.

Answers

Section Three — Assessment Tests

Pages 23-28 — Assessment Test 1

1) **D** — Lenny Scritch says he rested his "ladder against the wall of the enclosure" (line 5), suggesting the meerkats used it to climb out.

2) **B** — Lenny Scritch is described as "red-faced" (line 6), which suggests he is embarrassed.

3) **B** — The text mentions them visiting "Mill Lane Park" (line 9), a "pond" (line 9), "shops on Swan Street" (line 3) a "garden centre" (line 4) and an "indoor market" (line 4), but there is no mention of them visiting a wood.

4) **E** — "barking up the wrong tree" is an idiom that means 'taking the wrong approach'. In the text, people tried to trap the meerkats next to the pond, but this method didn't work and the meerkats escaped again.

5) **D** — The text mentions that they escaped from "a nearby safari park" (lines 2-3), they eat "caterpillars, grubs, bits of melon" (line 12), that they are "tunnelling through compost" (line 3) and that they have "tawny fur" (line 7). The size of meerkats' burrows isn't mentioned.

6) **B** — The text says that Kitty Chao "is familiar" with meerkats "having resided in southern Africa" (line 11).

7) **D** — The text says that "Snappy the turtle remains at large" (line 15), meaning it has not been recaptured.

8) **A** — You would find it in a newspaper because it is a news article.

9) **B** — 'daring' is closest in meaning to "audacious". Both words mean 'bold'.

10) **E** — 'chaos' is closest in meaning to "havoc". Both words mean 'complete confusion'.

11) **C** — 'corner' is closest in meaning to "ensnare". Both words mean 'to trap'.

12) **E** — "food" is a common noun because it is a general name for things that are eaten.

13) **C** — This is an example of alliteration because the 'p' sound is repeated at the beginning of "playful" and "posse".

14) **D** — They are adjectives because they describe nouns.

15) **C** — Sakura is trying to stop her garden being damaged by the movement of the bus, suggesting her fingers are trembling because she is worried.

16) **B** — Nathan gestures with his garden, causing pieces to come off, which suggests he's careless with it.

17) **D** — The text says that Sakura wanted to "ensure that nothing had become disordered" (line 7), showing that she wanted to examine her garden.

18) **A** — The garden contains "blue glass pebbles" (line 8) in the shape of a "stream" (line 9), a "tiny rockery" (line 8), "moss" (line 9), "wildflowers" (line 9) and "feathery ferns" (line 8), but it doesn't contain any actual feathers.

19) **B** — Sakura lets out her breath after checking her garden for damage. When she realises that it is "exquisite" (line 10), she relaxes, which suggests that she is relieved.

20) **D** — This phrase means that nobody else's miniature garden is as good as it, so Sakura thinks hers is the best.

21) **C** — There is no mention of Sally's shirt being stained.

22) **D** — Sakura thinks that the pebbles in her garden, which previously looked "brightly polished" (line 8), now look "dingy and lacklustre" (line 17), suggesting that she has lost confidence in her garden.

23) **D** — 'steady' is closest in meaning to "brace". Both words mean 'to stabilise'.

24) **B** — 'cautiously' is closest in meaning to "gingerly". Both words mean 'carefully'.

25) **A** — 'inspected' is closest in meaning to "scrutinised". Both words mean 'examined closely'.

26) **E** — "disordered" is an adjective here because it describes how "nothing" in Sakura's miniature garden was harmed.

27) **E** — The word "rattling" is onomatopoeia because it sounds like the noise it is describing.

28) **B** — This is a simile because the miniature gardens are compared to socks.

Answers

Pages 29-34 — Assessment Test 2

1) **B** — The text says that the national park covers "an overall area just shy of 9000 km²" (line 2). The phrase "just shy of" means 'just less than'.

2) **C** — The text mentions that Yellowstone is often viewed as "the world's first national park" (line 5), but also says that this is "not universally" (line 4) accepted. This suggests not everyone agrees that Yellowstone was the first national park in the world.

3) **C** — The word "continuously" means 'constantly', which shows scientists are monitoring the volcano all the time.

4) **B** — The text mentions that an eruption is "improbable in our lifetime" (lines 7-8), that eruptions happen "at roughly 700 000 year intervals" (line 7), that the volcano is currently "dormant" (line 6), and that it is in "Yellowstone National Park" (line 1). Although the text gives the approximate time between eruptions, it doesn't tell you when the volcano last erupted.

5) **A** — "concentric circles" are rings inside one another, and "vibrant hues" means 'bright colours', so the phrase refers to loops of bright colours.

6) **B** — The text describes "types of microorganism" that are able to live in the "hot water" (line 11) of hot springs. Microorganisms are 'tiny living things', such as bacteria.

7) **C** — Watching a geyser erupt is described as "a captivating display" (line 16), and "captivating" means 'gripping'.

8) **D** — Geysers are described as "a rare type of water feature" (line 13), which suggests they aren't very common.

9) **C** — The word "diverse" could most accurately be replaced by 'varied'. Both words mean 'made up of many different things'.

10) **B** — 'flourish' is closest in meaning to "thrive". Both words mean 'grow well'.

11) **E** — 'spectators' is closest in meaning to "observers". Both words mean 'people who watch something'.

12) **E** — This is an example of a metaphor because Yellowstone is described as being a gold mine.

13) **D** — "into" is a preposition because it tells you where the national park is in relation to Montana and Idaho.

14) **B** — This is an example of alliteration because the 's' sound is repeated at the beginning of "striking" and "scenery".

15) **D** — The text says that people in Shajarpur are "constantly boasting about the weather" (line 4), which suggests that they talk about how good the weather is all the time.

16) **C** — When the narrator gets off the flight they are "rumpled" (line 4) and "tired" (line 5). The word "rumpled" means 'dishevelled', which shows that their appearance is untidy. The word "tired" means 'weary'.

17) **C** — The narrator is unnecessarily specific about how long the fans are used for. This creates a mocking, sarcastic tone that pokes fun at the people of Shajarpur for boasting about their climate.

18) **E** — The text says that fans are used to "drive away the occasional fly" (lines 10-11). The phrase "drive away" means 'to encourage something to leave', which shows that fans are used to keep flies away.

19) **B** — Doctors in Shajarpur are described as "miserable because of their minuscule incomes" (line 16). The word "minuscule" means 'tiny', which suggests that doctors don't earn very much money.

20) **E** — The text mentions "cafes" on "terraces" (line 12), "lakes where birdwatchers would go birdwatching" (line 14), "Gardens" that "burst with blossoms" (line 12) and "tree-lined roadsides" (line 12). The text says that "citizens picnicked" (line 13), but it does not mention gardeners having picnics.

21) **C** — The text says that the climate in Shajarpur is "just right" in "summer", "winter" and "the monsoon" (lines 1-2), and goes on to say that the climate is "*gloriously* right in the spring" (line 2). This means that the weather in Shajarpur is best in the spring, not the summer.

22) **C** — The narrator mentions that many people "Like us" (line 24) are making Shajarpur "their new home" (line 24). This suggests that the narrator is going to live in Shajarpur.

23) **D** — "metaphorically" means 'figuratively'. Both words describe something imaginative rather than literal.

24) **B** — "beamed" could most accurately be replaced by 'grinned'. Both words mean 'to smile broadly'.

25) **B** — "thrilled" means 'delighted'. Both words mean 'very pleased'.

26) **A** — "pride" is an abstract noun because it is a name for something you can't experience with your five senses.

Answers

27) **B** — This is an example of personification because Shajarpur's climate is described as 'happy', which is a human emotion.

28) **E** — This is an example of alliteration because the 'b' sound is repeated at the beginning of "burst" and "blossoms".

Pages 35-40 — Assessment Test 3

1) **D** — If things "make your heart race", you find them exciting, so this phrase suggests the scenery and events may interest you.

2) **E** — The passage mentions "the town of Loiyangalani" (line 3), "the Marsabit region" (line 4), "Lake Turkana" (line 3) and "Kenya" (line 5), but it doesn't say where most visitors come from.

3) **A** — The text says that the festival takes place "over three days" (line 6), so it lasts for less than a week.

4) **C** — The text mentions the "bustle and excitement" (line 14) of the event, suggesting it is stimulating. It also says that it "includes something for everyone" (line 7), which suggests it is varied.

5) **B** — A "culture vulture" is someone who is interested in different aspects of art and culture.

6) **D** — The text mentions "marvelling at the skill of the local beadworkers" (line 10), spectating a "14-kilometre foot race" (line 13), eating "local dishes" (line 9) and listening to "traditional regional music" (line 8). The text doesn't mention visitors swimming in a lake.

7) **E** — The text says that the word comes "from the Swahili for 'beads'" (lines 10-11), the beads are used on "clothing, jewellery and accessories to enhance their beauty" (lines 11-12) and the beads are attached by "threading" (line 11), but it does not mention where the practice started.

8) **B** — You would be most likely to find this text in a travel brochure because it is trying to persuade the reader to visit the festival.

9) **B** — 'gripping' is closest in meaning to "riveting". Both words mean 'captivating'.

10) **A** — 'further' could most accurately replace "promote". Both words mean 'encourage'.

11) **A** — "under its belt" is an idiom. It is an informal expression that refers to something that has already been achieved.

12) **D** — This is an example of alliteration because the hard 'c' sound is repeated at the beginning of "cooperation" and "kinship".

13) **B** — This is a preposition because it tells you where the festival takes place in relation to the town.

14) **E** — "you" is a pronoun because it is used in place of a noun, the reader's name.

15) **D** — The text says that the email was sent to "the head of Imani's department" (lines 5-6), so Imani doesn't run the department.

16) **E** — The email was "classified" (line 5), which means it was secret.

17) **B** — The text says the department "dropped everything to concentrate on" (lines 8-9) the message, so they stopped working on other tasks.

18) **D** — A chore is a boring task, which suggests Imani's colleagues are finding the work boring.

19) **C** — The alien language "fascinated her" because it was "like nothing she'd ever encountered" (line 15). This means she hasn't seen a language like this before.

20) **A** — Imani thinks "The marks looked... half-finished" (lines 18-19), which means they look incomplete.

21) **B** — The plaque on Imani's door shows her last name is "Kirunda" (line 4).

22) **B** — Imani has a "triumphant smile" (line 22), which shows that she feels proud.

23) **A** — "esteemed" means 'well-respected'. Both words mean 'highly thought of'.

24) **E** — 'talent' is closest is meaning to "aptitude". Both words mean 'a natural gift'.

25) **D** — 'large' is closest in meaning to "extensive". Both words mean 'big'.

26) **E** — 'stubbornly' could most accurately replace "obstinately". Both words mean 'resisting change'.

27) **A** — This is an example of personification because smugness is a human emotion.

28) **D** — "sent" is a verb. It is the action word in this sentence.

Answers

Pages 41-46 — Assessment Test 4

1) **C** — Doxey Pool is in the south-west of the Peak District National Park, but not the south-west of the UK.

2) **B** — The passage says "the water level never drops significantly" (line 6), which means that the surface of the water always remains at about the same height.

3) **A** — The passage describes the pool as "modest in size" (line 5), meaning it is quite small.

4) **E** — The mermaid tries to "lure" (line 8) people into the water to "meet their end" (line 9), suggesting that she wants to drown them.

5) **B** — According to Florence Pettit, Jenny Greenteeth was "over seven metres tall" (line 13) and seemed to be "formed from water weed" (line 14), so she is huge and green.

6) **D** — The passage says that Florence went to the pool "before meeting a friend" (line 12), suggesting that she was alone at the pool.

7) **C** — The text suggests that the sighting may have been "authentic" (line 16) or the result of "imagination, deceit or an excess of sun" (lines 16-17), but it doesn't suggest Florence might have seen a branch covered in water weed.

8) **E** — The passage mentions the pool's "notoriety amongst uneasy locals" (line 17), suggesting they are wary of the pool.

9) **B** — 'apply' could most accurately replace "exercise". Both words mean 'to use'.

10) **E** — 'discourage' is closest in meaning to "deter". Both words mean 'to put off'.

11) **D** — 'evil' is closest in meaning to "malevolent". Both words mean 'having bad intentions'.

12) **C** — This is alliteration because the 's' sound is repeated at the beginning of "somewhat" and "sinister".

13) **B** — "cite" is a verb because it is an action word in this sentence.

14) **A** — "it" is a pronoun because it replaces the noun "being".

15) **D** — A "cause" can mean an 'aim', so the phrase means that you might have to put up with pain to achieve your goal.

16) **B** — The passage mentions the thief taking a "cake fork" (line 9), a "bracelet" (line 8), a "watch" (line 8), a "screwdriver" (line 9) and "pliers" (line 20), but it does not mention a padlock.

17) **E** — Each item is similar to something that the thief has already stolen (i.e. cutlery, a tool and jewellery), suggesting that Krista and Kurt believe these are items the thief wants to steal.

18) **C** — The text says that Krista finds Kurt's theory "far-fetched" (line 11), which means she thinks it is unlikely, and that this is because she can't think of a "possible function" (line 12) for the bracelet.

19) **A** — Krista scowls at Kurt after he "shuffled restlessly and sighed" (lines 15-16), which suggests she thinks the noise he is making might give away their hiding place.

20) **C** — Krista has heard a noise but she hasn't seen anything, which suggests that she moves and stretches her neck to try and see what made the noise.

21) **E** — The jackdaw is "ash-flecked" (line 20) and leaves a "sooty footprint" (line 21), suggesting it came in down the chimney. It then "vanished" (line 21) after flying to the fireplace, suggesting it went back up the chimney.

22) **A** — The passage says that Krista doesn't want the thief to "escape them once more" (line 6), which means they have tried to catch the thief before.

23) **B** — 'spoil' is closest in meaning to "bungle" — both words mean 'to ruin'.

24) **E** — 'naturally' is closest in meaning to "artlessly" — both words mean 'in a simple way'.

25) **A** — 'warning' is closest in meaning to "cautionary" — both words can mean 'intended to warn'.

26) **C** — This is personification because Krista's limbs "seek out" certain parts of the floor, which is a human behaviour.

27) **A** — This is a simile because it describes the noise as being like someone shaking an umbrella.

28) **C** — "from" is a preposition because it tells you where the snore began.

Answers

Pages 47-52 — Assessment Test 5

1) **D** — Archibald thinks resentfully about the stairs "snickering" (line 2), which suggests that he feels bitter about having to climb them. He is also "Mopping sweat from his forehead" (line 11), which suggests he is uncomfortable.

2) **B** — "Criminal" suggests that Archibald views the existence of stairs as wrong, which suggests that he thinks it is unfair that people have to use stairs.

3) **A** — Archibald sets down "the burden he'd been carrying" (line 7), which suggests he's moving something.

4) **E** — Archibald thinks "It was shameful that someone of his years" (line 7) should be climbing stairs, so he thinks he's too old for it.

5) **D** — The text mentions Archibald's "auburn whiskers" (lines 3-4), the "full moon" in the "black sky" (line 15), Archibald's desire to be "settling down for the night with a stiff drink" (lines 8-9) and that is is "November" (line 12), but doesn't mention why Archibald is in Egypt.

6) **A** — If something is described as a "jewel", it means it is viewed as being more special than things around it. This description suggests that Egypt is the most valuable country in the Orient.

7) **B** — The text says that Archibald has been visiting "For ten long years" (line 17), which is a decade.

8) **E** — When you have had your fill of something, it means you have had enough of it. This means that Archibald doesn't want to be in Egypt anymore.

9) **D** — 'ridiculous' is closest in meaning to "ludicrous". Both words mean 'foolish'.

10) **E** — "replica" means 'copy'. Both words mean 'a duplicate version of something'.

11) **B** — "fabled" could most accurately be replaced by 'legendary'. Both words mean 'relating to ancient stories'.

12) **A** — This is personification because laughing is something humans do, so the stairs are performing a human action.

13) **D** — This is a simile because the it describes the spout as being like a beak.

14) **C** — These are verbs because they are action words.

15) **A** — The text says that recycling "conserves crucial resources" (line 4), "cuts down on the pollution" (line 4), "offers employment" (line 4) and "generally uses less energy" than making new products "from scratch" (lines 5-6), but it doesn't mention anything about the cost.

16) **C** — The text says "people may not know what materials are actually recyclable" (lines 15-16).

17) **A** — The text says that paper is recycled with "ease" (line 7), which is one reason why is it widely recycled.

18) **D** — The text says that metal is "melted at very high temperatures and formed into bars" (lines 9-10), so it is heated and reshaped.

19) **E** — The author has "felt the shame" (line 12) of using "regular waste bins" (line 13), which suggests they feel guilty about their recycling habits.

20) **D** — The text says that "timber" (line 16) can be "taken to local recycling centres" (line 17) to be recycled. Timber means wood.

21) **A** — The text says "Paper and metal are the two most recycled materials in the UK" (line 7), so paper is recycled more than plastic in the UK.

22) **B** — The phrase "shouldn't lie solely with" means 'shouldn't only sit with', so the writer is suggesting that recycling is the responsibility of both individuals and organisations.

23) **B** — 'enormous' is closest in meaning to "colossal". Both words mean 'very big'.

24) **D** — "crucial" means 'essential'. Both words mean 'necessary'.

25) **A** — "contribute to" could most accurately be replaced by 'play a part in'. Both words mean 'be one of several factors that affect something'.

26) **B** — 'improve' is closest in meaning to "enhance". Both words mean 'make better'.

27) **E** — This is a rhetorical question because it's asking a question that you're not expected to answer.

28) **C** — "recyclable" is an adjective because it is describing the noun "materials".

Answers

Pages 53-58 — Assessment Test 6

1) **A** — The house is "on a grand scale" (lines 3-4) and has a "sweeping" (line 1) driveway covered in "gravel" (line 6).

2) **D** — The extract describes Kie's "Eyes widening" and says that he "swallowed heavily" (line 5), suggesting he is nervous. He then laughs and kicks at the drive, suggesting that he has overcome his nerves and feels more relaxed.

3) **B** — The passage says that "their irritating questions and tedious stories" (line 9) make Kie dislike old people.

4) **D** — The passage says that "Dad had insisted that he volunteer here" (lines 9-10).

5) **B** — The passage suggests that Kie "might have enjoyed" (line 11) volunteering to "plant trees", (line 10) whereas he doesn't want to help in the care home.

6) **E** — Before opening the door, Kie "glanced left and right" (line 14), suggesting he doesn't want anyone to see him.

7) **B** — The need to stifle a shocked noise suggests that Kie wasn't expecting what he saw in the room.

8) **C** — The residents are having a "vehement debate" (line 17) about how to make the cars in the computer game move faster.

9) **D** — 'abrupt' is closest in meaning to "terse". Both words mean 'brief'.

10) **A** — 'immaculate' is closest in meaning to "pristine". Both words mean 'perfect'.

11) **E** — "loitered" could be most accurately replaced with 'idled'. Both words can mean 'stood around'.

12) **B** — The word "crunched" is onomatopoeic because it sounds like the noise it describes.

13) **C** — The words are all adjectives because they describe nouns.

14) **E** — "rewild" is a verb because it is an action word in this sentence.

15) **B** — The first verse describes dawn, the second "noon" (line 8) and the third "twilight" (line 13), suggesting that a single day passes.

16) **D** — The poem mentions that "dawn's first cymbals" (line 1) are "Rousing the world" (line 2), but because dawn cannot actually play an instrument, this is a metaphor for the general sounds of early morning.

17) **B** — The poem says that people work "to forge a little gain" (line 4), which means that they want to make their lives better.

18) **E** — The men are "fasting" (line 5), which means 'refraining from eating'.

19) **A** — The poem mentions "cruel heat" (line 11) and the "radiance of noon" (line 8), meaning it is hot and bright.

20) **D** — The lovers drink "life's poignant sweet" (line 17) — this refers to them enjoying their evening together, not a physical drink.

21) **D** — The poem features farmers who "bind the mellowing grain" (line 3), shepherds who "tend the flock" (line 3) and bakers who sell "BREAD" (line 6). It doesn't mention the other jobs.

22) **C** — In the first verse, the "fasting men" (line 5) are hungry, so they desire the bread they can't have; in the second verse people desire fruit to quench their thirst in the "cruel heat" (line 11); and in the third verse they desire flowers to woo their "lovers" (line 16).

23) **C** — 'faint' is closest in meaning to "swoon" — both words mean 'to pass out'.

24) **A** — "Craves" could be most accurately replaced with 'desires' — both words mean 'to want very much'.

25) **D** — The shout "steals" down the street, which is "panting". These are both human behaviours.

26) **B** — The stars are described as a "canopy", so this is a metaphor.

27) **D** — "cry" and "toil" are nouns in this context because they are alternative names for 'shout' and 'work'.

28) **A** — "white" is an adjective because it describes the "roof-terraces".

Answers

Pages 59-64 — Assessment Test 7

1) **D** — The poem mentions the father urging his son to swim in the sea, that he stands on the shore clapping in support, and later in the poem that he watches his son swim in a pool. The father in the poem doesn't teach his son any swimming techniques.

2) **C** — Armbands are not mentioned in the poem.

3) **D** — Lines 5-8 mention that his lungs "seared and strained" (line 5) and that his teeth are "chattering" (line 7), so they focus on the physical sensation of being in the sea.

4) **C** — The "Waves" (line 2) are described as making the son feel "frozen" and "numb" (line 3), so the cold water is causing the "icy pain" (line 8).

5) **A** — The young son "found the waves' rhythm" (line 10) and "bobbed in time" (line 11) despite not being an experienced swimmer. This suggests that he has a natural feel for being in the water.

6) **E** — In the first half of the poem, the young son was "flailing" (line 6) in the water. In the second half of the poem, as an adult, he is "fearless" (line 15) and swims with "confident kicks" (line 17).

7) **A** — The son is now "full-grown" (line 15).

8) **C** — The sounds of the pool echo "within" (line 22) the son, which suggests that they have become part of him and he is very comfortable in the water.

9) **D** — 'induces' is closest in meaning to "prompts". Both words mean 'cause to happen'.

10) **B** — "arcs" could most accurately be replaced by 'curves'. Both words mean 'bends'.

11) **B** — 'indicator' is closest in meaning to "token". Both words mean 'a sign'.

12) **D** — "While" is a conjunction here. It tells you that the "kicks" (line 17) happen at the same time that the "lanes" (line 18) are channelling the swimmer.

13) **E** — This is personification because kissing is something that humans do, so the seawater is described as performing a human action.

14) **A** — "mewling" and "caws" are examples of onomatopoeia — the words sound like the noises they each describe.

15) **B** — The text says that Bogdan "knew" (line 4) he was cursed because "he'd not slept for two days" (line 4).

16) **E** — The text says the theatre is "everything Bogdan looked for" (line 9) because it is "empty, far from other dwellings" (lines 8-9), which means that no one lives there and it's far away from other people.

17) **D** — Bogdan "stole" (line 7) across the floor, and is described as "Stalking" (line 16) through the foyer. Both of these words relate to moving stealthily.

18) **C** — Bogdan has stolen a cursed jewel that causes him to suffer from bad dreams, and the theatre has a mosaic floor. There is no mention of any friend in the story.

19) **D** — The lines reveal that Bogdan regrets agreeing to his most recent theft. He thinks "he should not have taken the job" (line 25).

20) **C** — The text says that Bogdan "usually relished the night" (line 1) because it makes it easier to move around, has "sea-green" (line 16) eyes, prefers to stay "far from other dwellings" (line 9) and senses a "supernatural peril" (line 24). It doesn't mention him acting playfully.

21) **B** — The text describes the pouch as the "source of his woe" (line 17). This suggests that Bogdan thinks the gem is responsible for him being "*Cursed*" (line 4), so he wants to keep it away from him.

22) **A** — These lines describe the gem "Greedily" (line 20) swallowing the light, and say that its "ominous aura" (line 21) felt "seductive", "powerful" and "dark" (line 22). This creates a threatening mood because it makes the stone seem dangerous.

23) **E** — In this line, "prospect" is a noun — it is another name for 'idea'.

24) **C** — 'ready' is closest in meaning to "poised". Both words mean 'about to act'.

25) **D** — This is a metaphor because it describes Bogdan's sweat as rivers.

26) **A** — "dilapidated" could most accurately be replaced by 'crumbling'. Both words mean 'run-down'.

27) **E** — This is personification because the gem takes the light in "Greedily", and greed is a human quality.

28) **B** — This is an idiom: "a king's ransom" is 'a very large amount of money'.

Progress Chart

Use this chart to keep track of your scores for the Assessment Tests.

You can do each test more than once — download extra answer sheets from cgpbooks.co.uk/11plus/answer-sheets or scan the QR code on the right.

Answer
Sheets

	First Go	Second Go	Third Go
Test 1	Date: Score:	Date: Score:	Date: Score:
Test 2	Date: Score:	Date: Score:	Date: Score:
Test 3	Date: Score:	Date: Score:	Date: Score:
Test 4	Date: Score:	Date: Score:	Date: Score:
Test 5	Date: Score:	Date: Score:	Date: Score:
Test 6	Date: Score:	Date: Score:	Date: Score:
Test 7	Date: Score:	Date: Score:	Date: Score:

Look back at your scores once you've done all the Assessment Tests.
Each test is out of 28 marks.

Work out which kind of mark you scored most often:

0-16 marks — Go back to basics and work on your question technique.

17-23 marks — You're nearly there — go back over the questions you found tricky.

24-28 marks — You're a comprehension whizz.